# Science

*science fair*

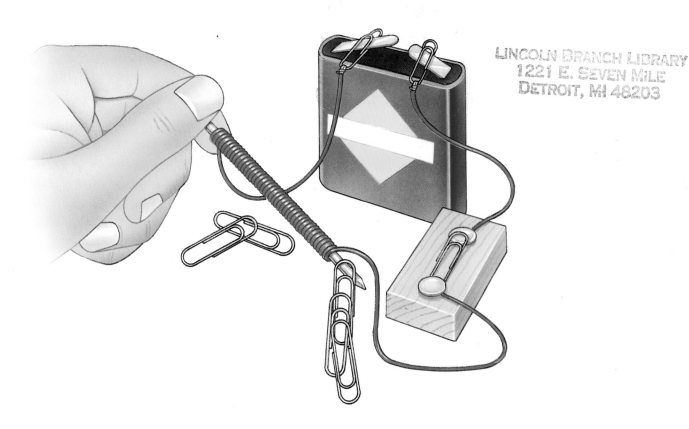

## DAVID GLOVER

### KING*f*ISHER

NEW YORK

# Contents

KINGFISHER
Larousse Kingfisher
  Chambers Inc.
80 Maiden Lane
New York, New York 10038
www.kingfisherpub.com

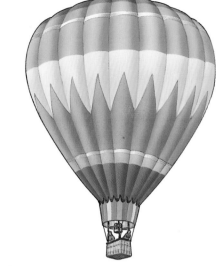

Material in this edition
previously published by
Kingfisher Publications Plc in
the *Young Discoverers* series.

This edition published in 2001

10 9 8 7 6 5 4 3 2 1

1TR/0701/WKT/-(MAR)/128MA

Copyright © Kingfisher
Publications Plc 2001

LIBRARY OF CONGRESS
CATALOGING-IN-PUBLICATION
DATA has been applied for.

ISBN 0-7534-5427-0

This edition produced by
PAGE*One*

Printed in China

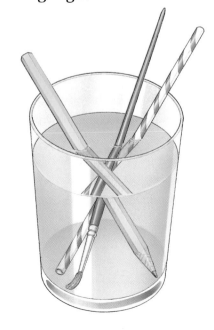

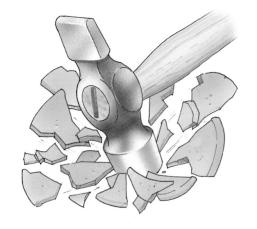

# About This Book

This book provides an all-round introduction to electricity and magnets, flight, energy, sound, light, and materials. It is filled with practical ideas and activities and suggests lots of experiments and things to look out for.

The first section, *Flying and Floating*, tells you about air and water—what they are and how we use their properties to fly planes or float boats.

*Sound and Light* tells you about sound and light—what they are and how we use them to hear and see.

*Batteries, Bulbs, and Wires* tells you about magnets, how to join batteries and wires to light up bulbs, and how electricity and magnets are linked.

*Solids and Liquids* is all about materials—the solids, liquids and gases from which everything around us is made.

You should be able to find nearly everything you need for the experiments around your home. You may have to buy some items, but they are all cheap and easy to find. Sometimes you will need to ask an adult for help, such as when drilling holes.

**Remember: Be a Smart Scientist**

- Before you begin an experiment, read the instructions carefully and collect all the things you need.

- Put on some old clothes or wear a smock.

- When you have finished, put everything away—especially sharp things like knives and scissors—and wash your hands.

- Keep a record of what you do and what you find out.

- If your results are not quite the same as those in this book, do not worry. See if you can work out what has happened and why.

# FLYING AND FLOATING

# Air and Water

Air and water are essential for life on Earth. Without air to breathe and water to drink we could not survive. But what exactly are air and water?

Air and water have different properties — they look, feel, and behave in different ways. Air is a gas. You can't see it or taste it but you can feel it when it blows over your face and hands. Water is usually a liquid, but it can also be a solid or a gas (see page 18).

Without water and air, all animals and plants would die. Animals use the oxygen gas from the air when they breathe in. Much of the oxygen in the air is replaced by green plants, which produce oxygen in their leaves when they make food.

After about 300 miles (500 km), the atmosphere starts to fade into space.

## The Atmosphere

The atmosphere is a layer of air around the Earth. It is often divided into four bands — the troposphere (nearest Earth), stratosphere, ionosphere, and exosphere.

Air is mostly made up of the two gases nitrogen (78%) and oxygen (21%). It also contains carbon dioxide gas (0.03%), water in the form of a gas (water vapor), and tiny bits of salt, dust, and dirt.

exosphere

ionosphere

stratosphere

troposphere

# Do it yourself

**Try these four simple experiments to compare the properties of air and water.**

Blow up one balloon and fill another with water, keeping it over the sink so you don't make a mess. To fill the water balloon, stretch the balloon's neck over the end of the faucet, then slowly turn on the water. Or you could use a funnel. Knot the end of each balloon.

**1.** First, hold one balloon in each hand to see which is the heavier. You'll find that the balloon filled with water is much heavier than the one filled with air.

**2.** Now squeeze each balloon. The air balloon will be quite firm and taut and will feel a little springy. The one filled with water will change shape as the water sloshes around inside.

**3.** Next, try sinking the balloons in water. You will be able to push the water-filled balloon under the water more easily than the air-filled balloon.

## Our Blue Planet

Over two-thirds of the Earth's surface is covered with water. Pictures of the whole Earth usually show the side with land, but from the other side our planet looks blue.

Pacific Ocean

**4.** Finally, stick a pin in each balloon. The air balloon will pop as the air rushes out, but the water balloon will simply sag as the water trickles away.

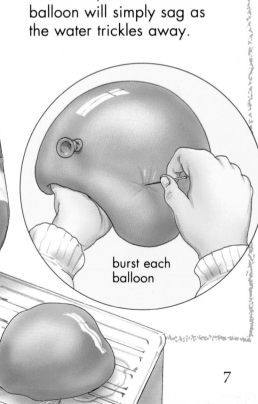

burst each balloon

# The Weight of Air

Air has weight, even though it seems thin and light. For example, the air inside a bus weighs as much as one of the passengers! Air is one thousand times lighter than water. This means that a bathful of air weighs about the same as a cupful of water. Air also takes up space — see how air bubbles fill the bottle in the experiment below.

## Blow It Up

When you pump up the tires on a bike, you're increasing the air pressure inside so that it can support both you and the bike (see next page).

## Do it yourself

**Here's a fun way to measure how much air your lungs hold (and find out more about the properties of air). You'll need a bowl, a large plastic bottle, and a long tube.**

**1.** Pour water into the bowl so it is three-fourths full. Then completely fill the bottle with water. Put your fingers over the top of the bottle so the water doesn't spill, turn it upside down and lower it into the bowl.

**2.** Thread the tube into the neck of the bottle. Then take a deep breath and blow down the tube.

## How It Works

Air is lighter than water, and it takes up space. As you blow, air bubbles rise up the tube and push the water out of the neck of the bottle into the bowl.

Can you fill the bottle with air?

The weight of all the air in the Earth's atmosphere pushes on everything with a force called air pressure. It may be hard to believe, but the air pressing on every square inch of your body weighs nearly 15 pounds! The reason you're not crushed by all that weight is because the air and liquids inside you push back with the same force.

## Eye-Spy

Have you ever sucked air from a plastic bottle or a thin metal can when you're drinking from it? Air pressure flattens the sides of the bottle or can slightly. The sides pop out again when you let air back in.

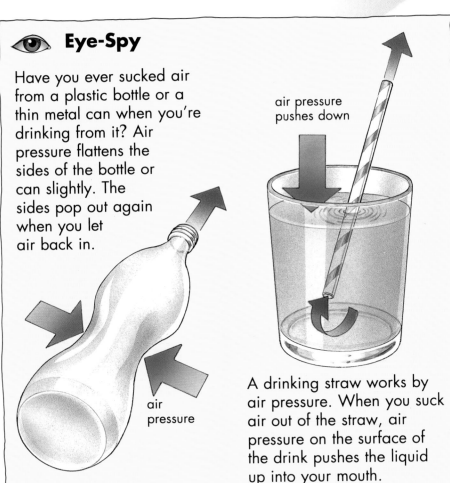

air pressure pushes down

air pressure

A drinking straw works by air pressure. When you suck air out of the straw, air pressure on the surface of the drink pushes the liquid up into your mouth.

Above: The amount of air in the atmosphere varies — the higher you go, the less there is. We describe this as the air getting thinner. Climbers of very high mountains, such as Mount Everest, must carry tanks of oxygen gas with them so they can still breathe.

# Hot Air

Have you ever wondered why smoke from a fire goes up into the air rather than spreading out? The reason is that hot air is lighter than cold air, so hot air rises.

Rising hot air is used to lift huge air balloons. A hot-air balloon is simply a large bag made out of a light material. The air inside a hot-air balloon is heated by a gas burner. This makes the balloon float up into the cooler atmosphere.

## Lighter Than Air

Some gases, such as helium, are lighter than air. This means that they don't need to be heated to help things fly. Helium-filled airships are used to film sports events such as the Olympic Games.

gas burner

# Do it yourself

## Make a hot-air pinwheel and balloon to see how hot air rises.

### Hot-Air Pinwheel

**1.** Cut out a circle of cardboard and make eight cuts, as shown. Twist up the edges slightly (so that air can rise through the gaps).

**2.** Push a pin through the middle of the cardboard to make a hole. Thread string through the hole and knot the end. (Make a large knot so the string doesn't slip through.)

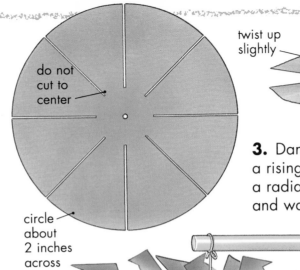

do not cut to center

circle about 2 inches across

twist up slightly

**3.** Dangle the pinwheel over a rising current of hot air (from a radiator, for example) — and watch it spin.

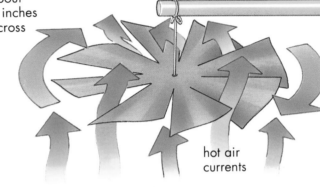

tie to a wooden stick or drinking straw

hot air currents

cut from tissue paper, 2 feet long

### Hot-Air Balloon

**1.** Cut out eight 2-foot-long pieces of tissue paper to the shape shown.

**2.** Glue the edges together to make a balloon shape. Don't use too much glue or your balloon will be too heavy.

**3.** Fill the balloon with hot air from a hair dryer. Does it fly? You could make a small tissue paper box and tie it to the bottom of the balloon to see whether the balloon can carry a load.

glue edges all around

hair dryer

11

# The Force of the Wind

When hot air rises, cool air usually flows in to take its place. This is what makes the wind blow. During the day, the Sun heats up parts of the land and the sea, which then warm the air above them. This warm air rises into the atmosphere and a stream of cooler air — the wind — blows in.

Winds carry seeds, make flags flap, and fill sails on boats. Strong winds can knock down trees and buildings.

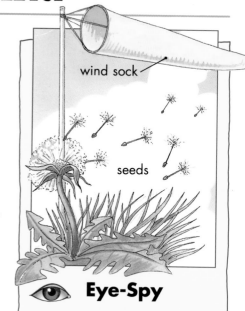

wind sock

seeds

## Beaufort Scale

In 1805, a British admiral called Sir Francis Beaufort introduced a scale to show the effect of different wind strengths on sailing ships at sea. Today, the Beaufort Scale describes the strength of the wind on land as well as at sea.

The scale has 12 numbers, ranging from calm to a violent hurricane.

### 👁 Eye-Spy

Look out for things that are moved by the push of the wind. Wind socks show which way the wind is blowing. Seeds are spread by the wind.

Force 0

**Calm**

smoke goes straight up

Force 1-3

**Light breeze**

leaves rustle; small branches move

Force 4-5

**Moderate wind**

small trees sway

Force 6-7

**Strong wind**

large trees sway

Force 8-9

**Gale**

shingles fall off roofs

Force 10-11

**Storm**

widespread damage

Force 12

**Hurricane**

disaster

Most things are heavier than air, so they do not float upward on a still day. But on a windy day, the wind can carry some lightweight things into the sky. This is how a kite works — it's lifted by the force of the wind.

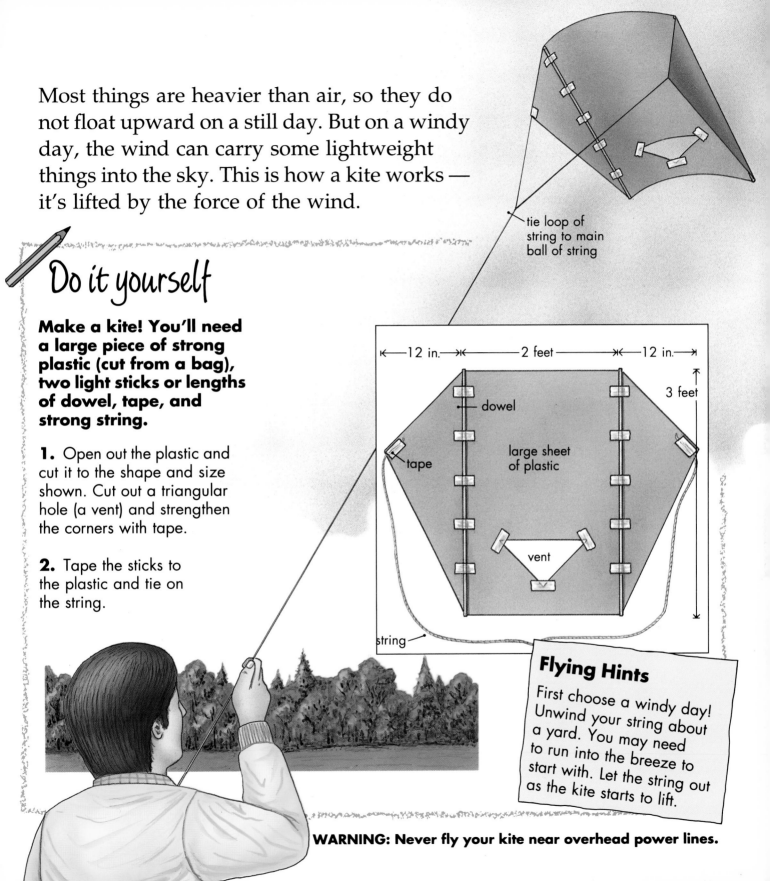

tie loop of string to main ball of string

# Do it yourself

**Make a kite! You'll need a large piece of strong plastic (cut from a bag), two light sticks or lengths of dowel, tape, and strong string.**

**1.** Open out the plastic and cut it to the shape and size shown. Cut out a triangular hole (a vent) and strengthen the corners with tape.

**2.** Tape the sticks to the plastic and tie on the string.

← 12 in. → ← 2 feet → ← 12 in. →

3 feet

dowel

tape

large sheet of plastic

vent

string

## Flying Hints

First choose a windy day! Unwind your string about a yard. You may need to run into the breeze to start with. Let the string out as the kite starts to lift.

**WARNING: Never fly your kite near overhead power lines.**

# Gliding Through the Air

Hot-air balloons and kites fly because they are lighter than air. But most aircraft are heavier than air. They need wings to help them to fly. Wings are a special shape — they're curved more above than below. They work when they move through the air at just the right angle. The flow of air above and below the wing makes a force called lift which keeps the aircraft in the air.

**1.** Many birds push themselves into the air by flapping their broad, flat wings. Some birds, such as gulls, soar and glide on moving air currents.

## Using Thermals

Thermals are created when dark surfaces, such as roads and fields, soak up heat from the Sun then pass on the heat to the air above. Gliders and soaring birds use these rising warm air currents to fly higher and stay airborne longer.

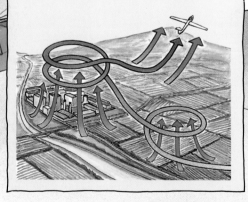

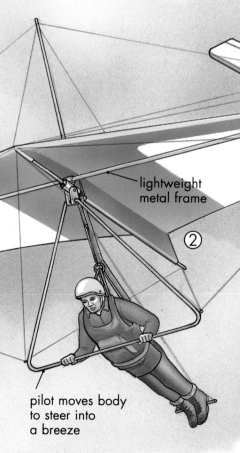

lightweight metal frame

②

pilot moves body to steer into a breeze

**2.** Hang gliders are usually launched by running down slopes or jumping off cliffs.

**3.** Gliders drift slowly downward at a gentle angle unless the pilot can find a rising air current to carry the lightweight glider up again.

When you cycle fast you can feel the air rushing past your body. But the faster you go the more the air drags you back. Modern cars and aircraft are smooth and rounded so that they pass through the air with as little drag, or air resistance, as possible.

**Check how the flow of air acts on a wing, making lift.**

**4.** Parachutes fall rather than fly. The open parachute fills with air and works like a brake, using the air's drag to slow itself down.

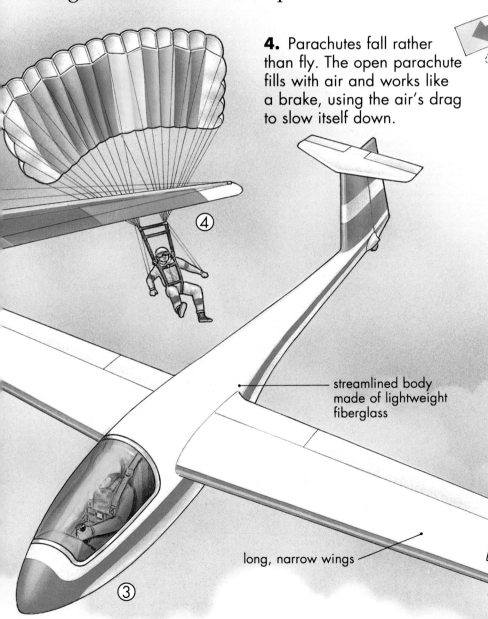

④

streamlined body made of lightweight fiberglass

long, narrow wings

③

Find a thin sheet of paper and hold it just under your lips. Blow hard over the paper and watch what happens.

You'll find that the paper will lift. The air you have blown over the paper moved faster and had less pressure than the air under the paper. This difference in air pressure made the paper lift.

### Staying Up

All aircraft with wings will only fly if they can move fast enough to keep air flowing around their wings (making lift). They also need enough lift to overcome their weight.

# Do it yourself

## Make a parachute!

**1.** Cut a square of plastic from a plastic bag or some fine, lightweight material. Make a small hole in the center. (This makes the parachute more stable.)

**2.** Tape a thread to each corner of the chute.

**3.** Tie the free ends of the threads together and tape the knot to a toy figure. Roll the chute into a ball and toss it into the air.

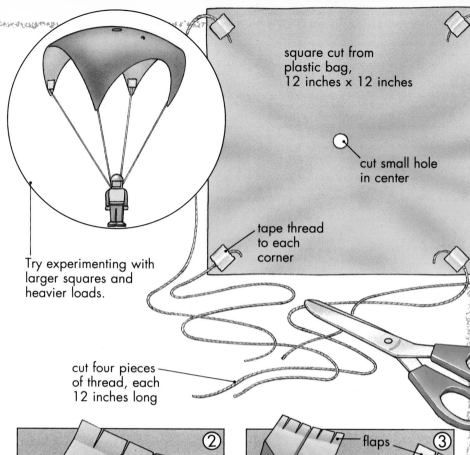

Try experimenting with larger squares and heavier loads.

square cut from plastic bag, 12 inches x 12 inches

cut small hole in center

tape thread to each corner

cut four pieces of thread, each 12 inches long

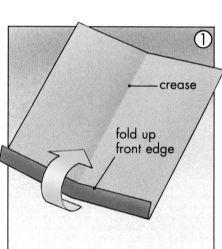

① crease

fold up front edge

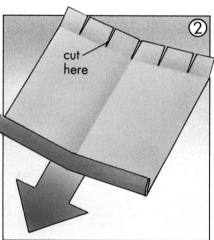

② cut here

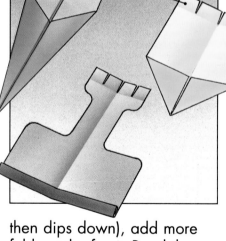

flaps ③

## Fly a superglider!

**1.** Fold a sheet of rectangular paper in half, making a neat, stiff crease down the middle. Fold up the front edge two or three times.

**2.** Fold the back edge once and make a series of cuts (for (flaps), as shown. Launch the glider into the air. If it falls too fast, unfold some of the paper from the front. If it stalls (tips up at the front

then dips down), add more folds at the front. Bend the flaps to see how they change the glider's flight.

**3.** Try some of these glider shapes or design your own.

# Planes and Helicopters

Gliders and hang gliders must go where air currents take them, but aircraft with engines can travel where the pilot wishes, and they can keep going until they run out of fuel. Engines keep an airplane pushing through the air so that its wings are working, creating lift.

Helicopters are different because they can fly backward, forward, and up and down. They create lift by pushing down on the air. Tilting the blades moves the helicopter in different directions.

Because they can hover, helicopters are useful for watching traffic, lifting loads, or rescuing people from the sea or from mountainsides.

## Do it yourself

**Make a helicopter rotor.**

**1.** Carefully cut a rectangular strip from a plastic bottle.

**2.** Cut two slits, one on each side of the strip, as shown.

**3.** Make a small hole in the middle of the strip and push a pencil through so that it's a tight fit.

**4.** Hold the pencil between the palms of your hands, spin it quickly and let go.

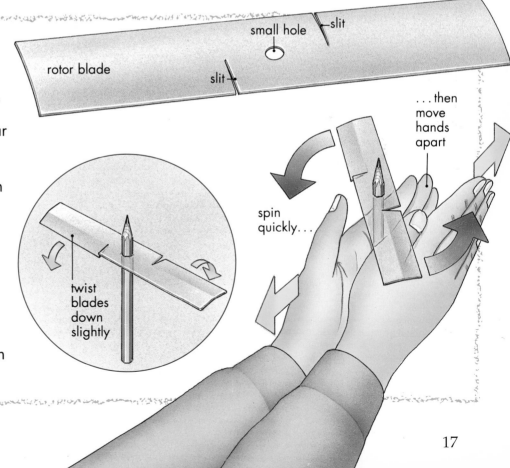

rotor blade

small hole

slit

slit

twist blades down slightly

spin quickly . . .

. . . then move hands apart

# A Watery World

We drink it, we wash with it, we swim in it — water is very special. Without water, our Earth would be a dry, lifeless desert. Water can exist in three different forms — as a liquid, as a gas (called water vapor), and as a solid (ice), and we use all three forms of water in our everyday lives. For example, steam irons use the gas from boiling water to press clothes, and we have iced drinks to keep cool.

gas

liquid

solid

Water freezes at 32°F (0°C) and boils at 212°F (100°C). Steam is a cloud of water droplets. Steam spurts from a boiling kettle because it takes up more space than the liquid.

## Frozen Solid

Solid water forms in two different ways. Ice is made when liquid water cools to 32°F (0°C). This temperature is called water's "freezing point."

The second way is when water vapor freezes to make frost. For example, dew may freeze into frost on cold mornings.

clouds are water vapor

snow is frozen water

water vapor turns into steam in cold air

ice is frozen water

Gravity, the invisible force that pulls everything toward the center of the Earth, pulls on water too. In places where it cannot flow through surface rocks, water forms rivers, lakes, and oceans. In other places, different kinds of rock let the water seep through. All water on Earth eventually settles at the lowest level that it can possibly reach.

This photograph shows a waterfall in Ethiopia, Africa.

# Do it yourself

**See how the surface of water in any container is always level, no matter which way you tip it up. You'll need two clear plastic bottles with tops and a plastic tube.**

**1.** Fill one of the bottles with water and screw on the top.

**2.** Connect the bottles with the plastic tube (like the kind used in wine-making). Use shampoo or ketchup

bottles with nozzles, over which you can push the tube, or ask an adult to make holes through the bottle tops for you.

**3.** Turn the bottles upside down. Make a small hole in the bottom of each bottle to let the air in and out. Now change the height of the bottles and compare the water levels.

## How It Works

You'll find that no matter where you hold the bottles, the water will flow from one to the other until the level of water is the same in them both.

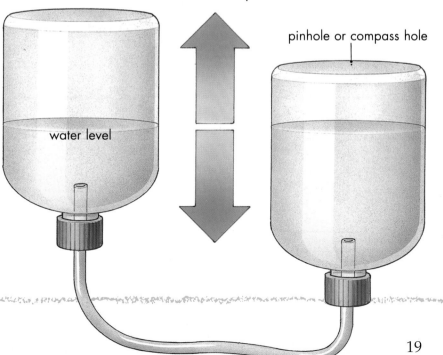

water level

pinhole or compass hole

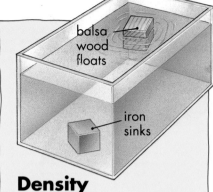

# Floating and Sinking

Have you ever wondered why some things float on water while other things sink? A plastic ball will float, for example, but a stone will sink at once.

Whether something floats or sinks depends on its density (how heavy it is for its size), and its shape. The shape of an object controls how much water it pushes out of the way, or displaces. A plastic ball floats because it is lighter than water. It cannot displace much water with its weight. A stone is heavier than water so its weight pulls it under.

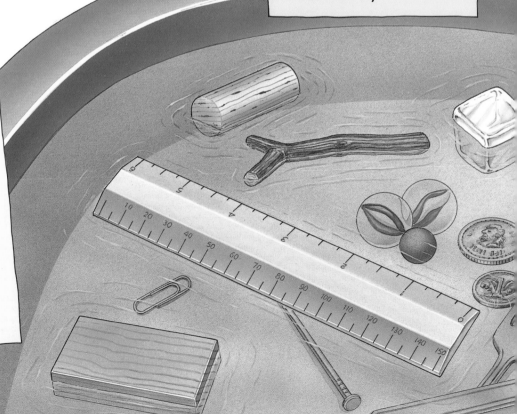

balsa wood floats

iron sinks

## Density

A cube of iron is 7 times heavier than a cube of water the same size. But a cube of balsa wood is 5 times lighter than the water. If something is heavy for its size we say it has a high density. If it is light for its size, it has a low density.

## 👁 Eye-Spy

Next time you have a bath, see how far the water level rises as you lower your body into the water. This will show you how much water you displace!

# Do it yourself

**Experiment with different materials to see whether they float or sink. Then try changing sinkers to floaters.**

First test a collection of solid objects, such as things made of metal, wood, glass and plastic.

You'll find that small, heavy objects, such as coins and marbles, will sink. Larger, light things, such as a stick or a cork, will float.

Next, scrunch up a sheet of aluminum foil into a tight ball and drop it into the water. The ball will sink because it's heavier than the water it displaces.

Now fold another sheet of foil into a boat shape. Does it float or sink now?

Try the same experiment with a ball of modeling clay.

## How It Works

The wide, flat boat shape displaces more water than the solid ball made from the same material. Most of the boat is actually filled with air. Together, the boat and the air inside it are lighter than the water they displace and so the boat floats.

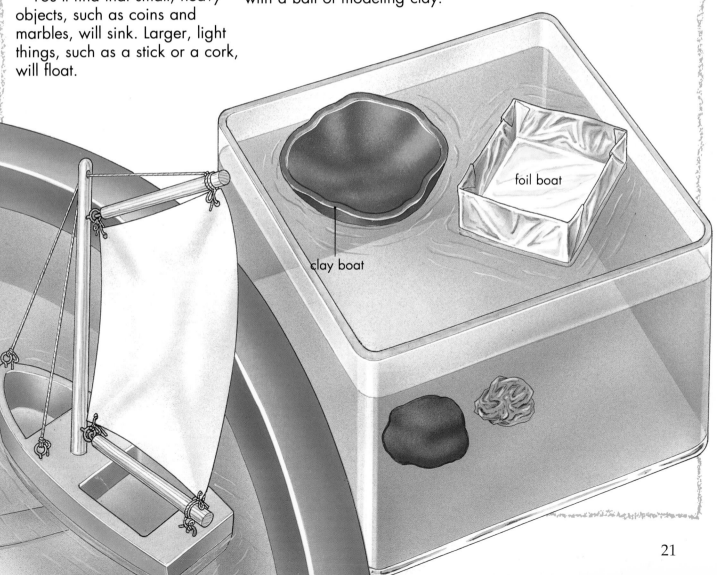

clay boat

foil boat

21

Sometimes boats capsize —
they turn on their sides and fill
with water. To reduce this risk,
a boat must be made to
the right shape and its cargo
must be loaded correctly so
that the boat is balanced.

Container ships like the one
on the right are designed to
carry heavy loads.

# Do it yourself

**See which boat designs
are best at carrying
cargo safely.**

foil tray

marbles

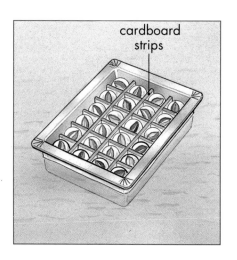

cardboard
strips

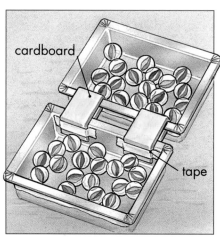

cardboard

tape

**1.** Float a foil dish on some
water. Add some marbles
one at a time for the cargo.
You'll find that the marbles
roll around in the boat until
they tip it over altogether.

**2.** Divide up the inside with
strips of cardboard to make
the cargo more stable. Large
container ships, like the one
in the photograph above, are
divided in a similar way.

**3.** Tape two foil trays side by
side and balance the cargo
again. This boat design is
called a catamaran. It is a
very stable design and will
not capsize easily.

# A Stretchy Skin

Have you ever noticed how water collects into tiny drops on a polished car or on shiny shoes? The weight of the water tries to make it flow and spread, but water has a kind of stretchy elastic skin that holds it together.

Fill a glass right up to the top with water. Can you see how the water's surface bulges slightly over the brim of the glass? The force holding the water together is surface tension.

Some lightweight animals, such as this spider, use surface tension to walk on water.

## Do it yourself

**A metal needle has a higher density than water and should sink, but you can make it float on water's stretchy skin.**

Slowly slide the needle across the rim of a filled glass, onto the water's surface. Be careful not to break the surface tension. If you find this hard, try floating the needle on a raft of tissue paper. The paper will become waterlogged and sink, leaving the needle floating on the water.

Look closely — you'll be able to see how the water's skin flexes under the weight of the needle.

### More Things to Try

Add one or two drops of liquid soap to the water. You'll find that the needle will soon drop to the bottom of the glass as the soap weakens the water's surface tension.

# Puddles and Clouds

Next time it rains, wait for the rain to stop, then go out and see how long it takes for the rain puddles to disappear. Some of the water in puddles soaks down into the ground, but the rest dries up into the air. The Sun's heat makes the water turn into the gas we call water vapor. This process is called evaporation.

Water evaporates more quickly when there is a breeze blowing than when the air is still. That's why laundry hung outside dries faster on a windy day than a still one.

You can sometimes see water vapor rising from a damp dog as it lies steaming in the sunshine on a hot day.

## Do it yourself

**Investigate how quickly water evaporates.**

Find three cloths of equal size. Soak them in water, then leave them in different places to dry:

**1.** Hang the first on a line.

**2.** Leave the second screwed up in a bowl.

**3.** Lay the third flat on the ground.

① ② ③

Which one dries the fastest?

### How It Works

The towel on the line will dry the fastest because the water vapor can escape from it more easily. If there's a breeze to carry the vapor away, the towel will dry even more quickly.

## Condensation

Water vapor in the air can turn back into liquid water, too. This happens when warm air cools down. As cold air cannot hold as much water vapor as warm air, some of the water vapor forms tiny drops of liquid. This process of gas turning back into liquid is called condensation.

There is water vapor in the air you breathe out. If you breathe onto a cold glass mirror, some of the vapor in your breath condenses into a mist of tiny water droplets.

**Eye-Spy**

Watch out for water vapor condensing. You can often see it on the cool windows of a warm room, on the mirror of a steamy bathroom, or on the inside of a greenhouse. Plants give off water vapor at night (with carbon dioxide gas), which condenses on the greenhouse's cool glass.

# Do it yourself

**Leave some glasses in a freezer for about two minutes. When you bring them out, see how water vapor from the air condenses on their sides.**

Below: Clouds are made from water vapor. When warm air rises, it eventually cools and the water vapor condenses into a mist of droplets. If the droplets get large enough, they fall from the sky and it rains.

# Water Power

We can use the power of moving water just as we can use wind power. Turning water wheels were once used to grind corn or to drive tools such as drills. Today, water power is used mostly to make electricity. Water is stored in huge reservoirs behind dams. When it is released, the force of the falling water drives turbines which produce electrical power.

## Water Wheels

Water wheels like this one were first built over two hundred years ago. This photograph shows a working wheel in Syria.

# Do it yourself

### Build a water wheel.

**1.** Ask an adult to help you make a hole through the middle of a cork and cut eight slots in its sides.

**2.** Glue a plastic spoon in each slot. When the glue is dry, slide a knitting needle through the hole in the cork.

**3.** To work the wheel, hold it under a stream of gently running water.

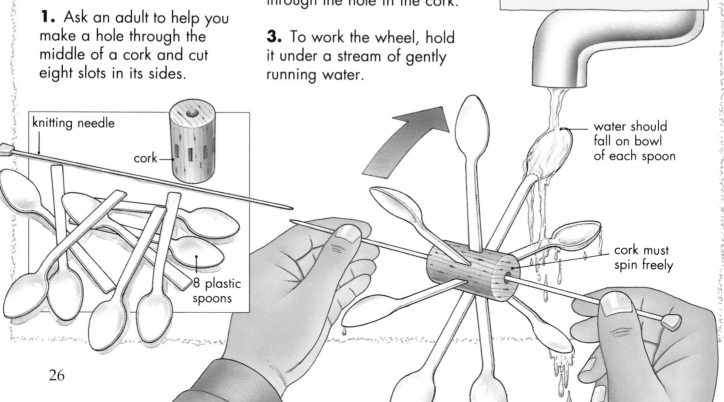

knitting needle

cork

8 plastic spoons

water should fall on bowl of each spoon

cork must spin freely

26

# SOUND AND LIGHT

# Thunder and Lightning

Have you ever been caught in a thunderstorm? First you see a flash of lightning, then you hear a crash of thunder. The sky is filled with light and sound.

Lightning flashes are huge sparks of electricity. They are so powerful they can be seen a long way from a storm. Light travels very fast, so we see the flash of light in the same second that it is made. But sound travels more slowly. It may be several seconds before the sound of a thunderclap reaches our ears.

The Vikings believed that thunder was the sound of their god, Odin, hammering his sword ready for war.

## How Far Is the Storm?

Light travels a million times faster than sound, so it arrives almost instantly. But sound takes about 5 seconds to travel 1 mile.

You can work out how far a thunderstorm is from you by timing the number of seconds between seeing a lightning flash and hearing the roll of thunder.

If you count $2\frac{1}{2}$ seconds, then the storm is half a mile away, 5 seconds means that it is 1 mile away, 10 seconds 2 miles, and so on.

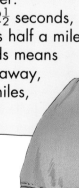

Look out for light arriving before you hear sound. For example, next time you go to a firework display, see if you can see the rockets exploding before you hear the bangs.

The giant sparks of electricity given off by lightning can strike tall trees and set them on fire. So **never** shelter under a tree during a thunderstorm.

In cities, many tall buildings have lightning rods running down their sides. These metal rods carry the electricity safely down the buildings into the ground.

# Sound Waves

If you flick the end of a rope up and down, the "flick" travels along the rope like a wave — the section of rope in your hand passes the movement on to the next section, which passes it on again, and so on. This is how sound travels through the air. When you burst a balloon, the escaping air gives a sudden push to the air around it. This push is passed on through the air like the wave traveling along the rope and we hear the loud bang, or pop, when the sound wave reaches our ears.

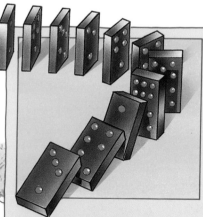

## Making a Bang

Bursting an air-filled paper bag forces the air trapped inside the bag through the hole in the paper. This sends a powerful sound wave through the air that reaches our ears as a loud bang.

Tie a rope to a tree or to a lamppost and flick the free end up and down to see how waves move along the rope.

## Passing It On

Set up a row of dominoes, spacing them fairly close together. Now knock the first one over and watch how the wave travels down the line.

# Do it yourself

**Build a sound cannon so you can see a sound wave make a candle flicker. You will need a cardboard tube, some plastic, scissors, tape, a small candle, a saucer, and some sand.**

**1.** Stretch the pieces of plastic tightly across each end of the cardboard tube and tape them firmly in place.

**2.** Make a small hole in the middle of the plastic at one end of the tube.

tape firmly in place or use rubber bands

plastic cut from plastic bag

**3.** Put some sand in the saucer and stand the candle upright in it. Ask an adult to light the candle for you.

**4.** Hold the end of the tube with the hole in it about an inch away from the flame.

## Noisiest Explosion

When the Indonesian island of Krakatoa exploded in 1883, the sound wave was heard in Australia, 2,500 miles away.

**5.** Tap the other end of the tube with your finger. Watch what happens to the flame.

## How It Works

When you tap the plastic, you make a sound wave that travels down the tube and out of the hole at the end. The wave can be strong enough to blow out the candle flame.

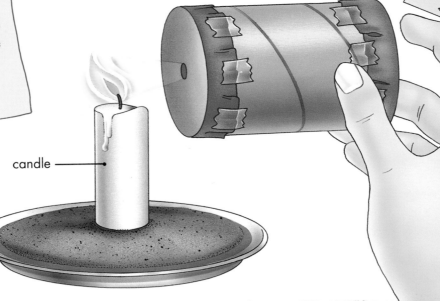

candle

saucer filled with sand or soil

# Feeling Sound

If you bend the end of a ruler over the edge of a table and then let it go, the ruler will move up and down. When something moves quickly back and forth like this, we say that it is vibrating.

Try changing the length of the ruler on the table. The shorter the length over the edge, the quicker the vibrations and the higher the sound. We call the number of sound waves a second, the *frequency* of the waves.

Nearly every sound you hear is made by something vibrating.

## Feeling Vibrations

When something is making a steady sound it must be vibrating to push the air around it back and forth. If you hold your hand against things making sounds you can usually feel the vibrations. Here are some things to test:
- a purring cat
- a ringing telephone
- your throat when you are singing
- a radio playing loud music

## Seeing Vibrations

We cannot see sound waves, but sometimes we can see the vibrations that make sounds. Sprinkle a few grains of uncooked rice on some paper, lay it over a radio and watch the rice jump!

turn up sound

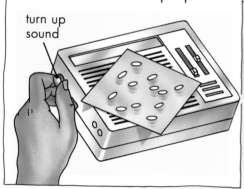

press this end down firmly

32

If you stretch a rubber band between your fingers and twang it, it vibrates and makes a quiet sound. The sound isn't very loud because the band is small and it can only push a small amount of air. To make the sound louder we must amplify it. In other words, we must make the vibrations of the elastic band push more air to and fro.

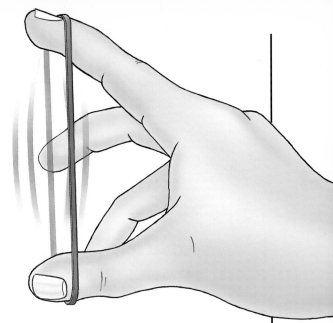

# Do it yourself

**Make a sound amplifier. You will need a large plastic mixing bowl, a sheet of plastic cut from a plastic bag, tape, scissors, and two rubber bands.**

**1.** Stretch the plastic tightly over the top of the bowl, like the skin of a drum. Secure the plastic with a rubber band and tape.

**2.** Tape the other rubber band to the middle of the plastic.

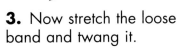

**3.** Now stretch the loose band and twang it.

## How It Works

When the band vibrates it makes the stretched plastic vibrate. Because the plastic sheet is much bigger than the elastic band, it pushes a lot more air and amplifies the sound. That's why a jack-hammer makes a very loud noise — it vibrates the ground around it.

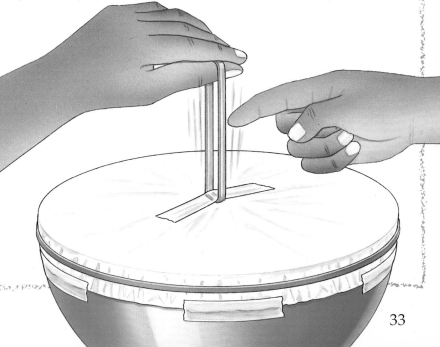

33

# Making Music

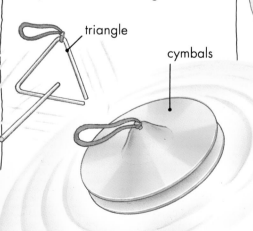

All musical instruments use vibrations to make sounds. Stringed instruments, like guitars, have stretched strings that vibrate when they are plucked or strummed. Wind instruments, like recorders or clarinets, make vibrations when the musician blows down the tube. Percussion instruments, like drums, triangles, and cymbals, are usually played by hitting or tapping them to make them vibrate.

## Moving Air

Because a triangle only moves a small amount of air, it makes a quiet sound. The cymbals are bigger and move a lot more air. So they make a loud sound when they are crashed together.

triangle

cymbals

body vibrates, amplifying the sound

sound hole

body

strings

### 👁 Eye-Spy

When you see an orchestra playing, see if you can pick out the sounds of different instruments.

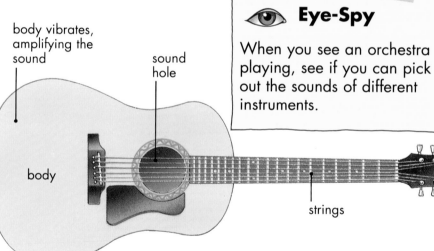

funnel-shape amplifies the sound

The trumpet is a brass instrument. The player makes sounds by vibrating her lips.

# Do it yourself

## Make your own musical instruments.

**1.** Make a trumpet with a short piece of hose and a funnel. When you blow into it, try to vibrate your lips — it takes lots of practice to get a clear note.

**2.** Try blowing over the top of an empty bottle. If you fill several bottles with different amounts of water, you can get high and low notes. Or you could blow sharply over a pen top to make a high, piercing whistle.

**3.** Make a rich, deep note with a string bass like the one in the picture. Ask an adult to drill a hole in one end of the pole so you can thread string through it. Knot the string tightly under the top of the box and pluck it. Cut a hole in the box to make the sound louder.

**4.** Tap small cans, large pans, big, empty boxes, or glass jars with pens, spoons, or anything else you can find. Some things will make dull sounds that fade quickly. Others vibrate for longer and make bright sounds that ring on.

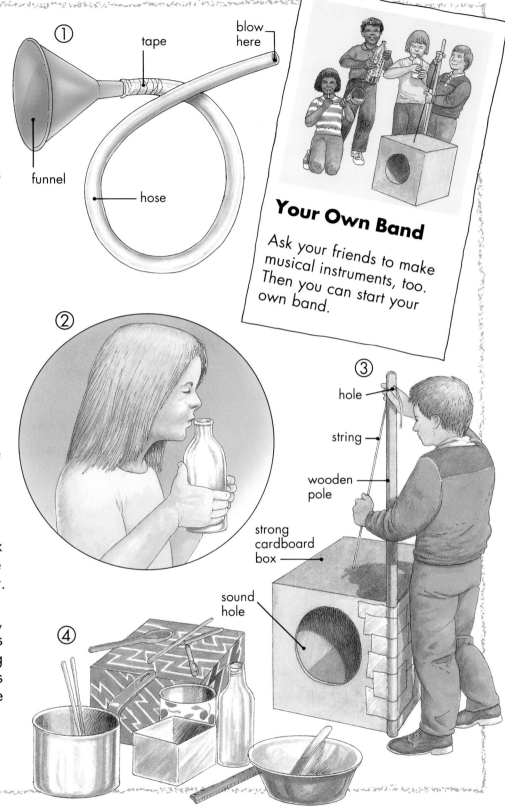

① tape — blow here — funnel — hose

**Your Own Band**

Ask your friends to make musical instruments, too. Then you can start your own band.

②

③ hole — string — wooden pole — strong cardboard box — sound hole

④

# How Do You Hear?

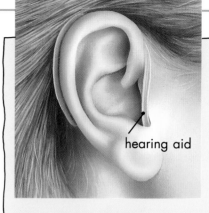

The drawing below shows what the inside of your ear looks like. The part outside your head catches sounds. Inside, there is a small piece of skin stretched tight like the skin on a drum. This is called the eardrum. When sounds enter your ear, they make the eardrum vibrate. The vibrations are amplified and are picked up by nerves. The nerves then send signals about the sound to your brain and you "hear."

hearing aid

## Hearing Aids

Some people can't hear very well because their ears have been damaged. Hearing aids are tiny electrical amplifiers that pick up and amplify sounds as they enter the ear.

## How Loud is Loud?

The loudness of a sound is measured in decibels (dB for short). Sounds over 100 dB can damage your ears.

- Airplane 100-150 dB
- Jackhammer 100 dB
- Loud music 90-95dB
- Talking 40-60 dB
- Whispering 20 dB
- Falling leaves 10 dB

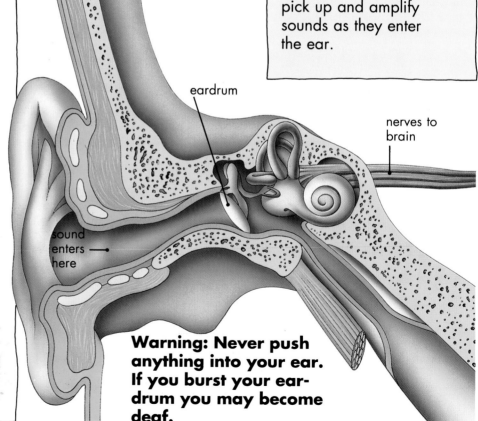

eardrum

nerves to brain

sound enters here

earmuffs to protect ears

**Warning: Never push anything into your ear. If you burst your eardrum you may become deaf.**

# Do it yourself

## Can you tell which direction sounds are coming from?

**1.** Put on a blindfold and ask a friend to make a sound, sometimes from behind you and sometimes to the right or left.

**2.** Try pointing in the direction of the sound each time. You could experiment with different sounds (like humming) and distances.

whistle

point at direction sound is coming from

blindfold

**3.** Try blocking one ear. Does this make it easier or more difficult to tell the direction of the sound?

### 👁 Eye-Spy

Watch for animals using their ears. Hares can twist their long ears around so they can check where a sound is coming from. Sometimes you can see birds tilting their heads toward sounds, too.

# Light Waves

Without light from the Sun, the Earth would be a dark, cold, lifeless place. Light is a kind of energy. We use light to see. Plants use it to grow.

Like sound, light travels in waves. But light does not need to travel through air or water. It can pass through empty space where there is no air or water to carry it. Light waves travel in straight lines, but they travel so fast we can't see them move. We just see a straight, steady beam of light.

## First Light Bulb

The first electric light was invented by Thomas Edison in 1879. He used electricity to heat a piece of burnt thread so it glowed brightly.

## Light All Around

We need light to be able to see. During the day, we get light from the Sun. At night, or in a dark room, we use artificial light, such as light from electric light bulbs.

When you read a book by sunlight or by lamplight, the light is reflected from the pages of the book into your eyes. Different things reflect different amounts of light. That is why some things look shiny and bright and others look dull.

# Do it yourself

**See for yourself how light travels in straight lines. You will need a bright flashlight and some cardboard.**

**1.** Cut out three pieces of cardboard the same size and make a small hole in the center of each of them.

## Straight Beams

Sometimes, rays of sunlight are broken up by trees or clouds. You can then see that the light rays are straight.

**2.** Line up the cards so you can see the light shining through the holes. (You could support them in modeling clay or ask a friend to help.)

**3.** Now move the middle card from side to side. You will only be able to see the light when the three holes are in a straight line.

look here

# Look in the Mirror

When light hits a surface, the light rays are reflected, or bounced back. Flat, shiny surfaces reflect light best. That's why mirrors are made of flat, highly polished glass with a shiny silver coating on the back. When you look in a mirror you can see a reflection of yourself. Mirrors can be used to change the direction of light to see into awkward spots — like a dentist looking at your back teeth!

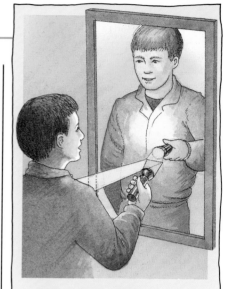

### 👁 Eye-Spy

If you shine a flashlight into a mirror you can see how the mirror reflects the beam of light.

## Do it yourself

**Find one or two small mirrors and try these different ways of reflecting light.**

**1.** Can you read the numbers? You could practice mirror writing and send secret messages to your friends.

① 9243

place mirror on blue line

②

③

**2.** Catch the Sun's light and send signals.

**3.** See around corners.

**4.** Make kaleidoscope patterns. (Place a mirror on each line.)

④

Note: Never look directly at the Sun, even when it is reflected in a mirror.

# Do it yourself

**Make a periscope to look over the heads of a crowd of people or to peep over a wall.**

**1.** Cut out two holes of the same size at the top and bottom of an empty juice or milk carton. One hole must be on each side.

**2.** Measure and draw two squares on both sides of each hole and divide the squares with diagonal lines. This is to help you make sure that the mirrors are at the same angle of 45°. Ask an adult to help.

**3.** Cut out two diagonal slits on each side, as shown. They should be just big enough to slide your mirrors through.

**4.** Slip the mirrors in place with the reflecting sides facing each other.

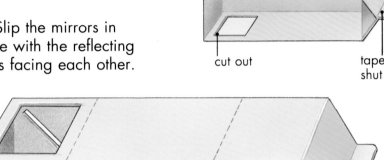

cardboard carton

mirrors (same size)

cut out

cut out

tape shut

45°    draw lines to get correct position for the slits    45°

mark and cut slits

The picture below shows how the mirrors change the direction of light. Light hits the top mirror and is reflected down to the bottom mirror and then into your eyes.

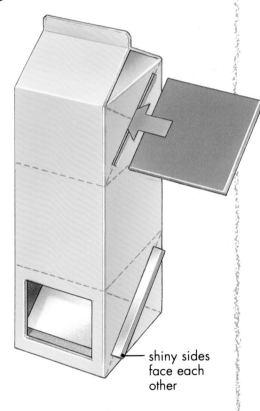

shiny sides face each other

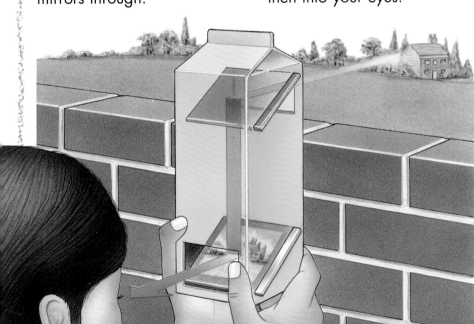

# How Lenses Work

Lenses are pieces of glass or clear plastic that are specially curved to bend light by refraction. If you look through a concave lens, things look smaller. Convex lenses can make things look bigger. Magnifying glasses and microscopes have convex lenses.

The lenses in eyeglasses help people see more clearly. We say that people who wear glasses with concave lenses are near-sighted, and people who wear glasses with convex lenses are farsighted.

## Eye-Spy

Do you or your friends wear glasses? Are the glasses concave or convex? The box on the next page tells you how to test them.

## Do it yourself

**Make a simple magnifier to make things look bigger.**

**1.** Cut a hole in a piece of cardboard or use a slide mount.

**2.** Cover the hole with clear plastic tape and use a pencil to drip a single drop of water over it. The rounded droplet should magnify things slightly.

You could also try looking at things through the bottom of a thick glass or a glass filled with water.

clear tape

## Testing Lenses

Collect some old pairs of glasses. First, look at some print in a book. If the words look smaller, the lenses are concave. If they look bigger, the lenses are convex.

Another test for lenses is to look at the shadows they cast on a sheet of paper. Concave lenses spread the light so they cast a big, dark shadow. Convex lenses concentrate the light. Their shadow is small and bright.

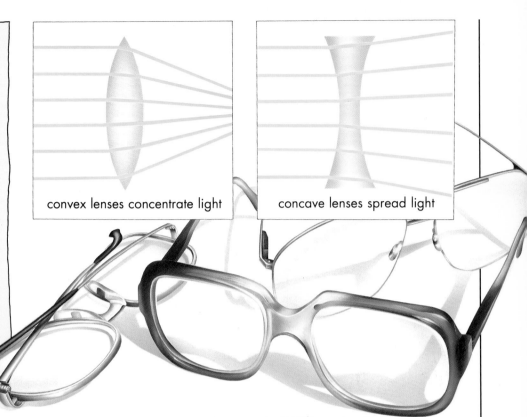

convex lenses concentrate light

concave lenses spread light

# Do it yourself

**Try this experiment with a convex lens from an old pair of reading glasses or a magnifying glass to see how it concentrates light.**

Stand opposite a sunny window and move your lens toward a sheet of white paper until you can see an image of the window and the scene outside. The image will be upside down. The lenses in your eyes work in a similar way. Look at the box at the bottom of the next page.

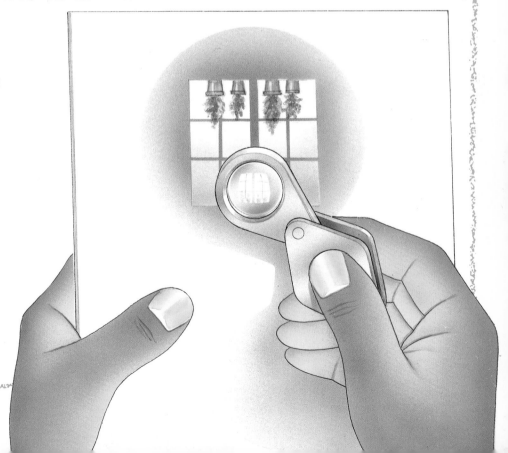

# How Do You See?

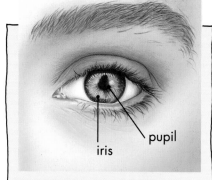

iris    pupil

**Looking at Eyes**

Look at your eyes in a mirror. Close them. Count to 20. Open your eyes. Your pupils will be larger to let in more light.

Look at your eyes in a mirror. The black spot in the middle is called the pupil. The colored part around the pupil is the iris. The size of the iris changes to make the pupil bigger or smaller. In very bright light the pupil gets smaller so you are not dazzled. In dim light the pupil gets larger to let more light into your eye. If you go into a dark room after being in strong sunlight you can't see much at first. But after a while your eyes adjust and you can see more clearly.

## How Eyes Work

The lens collects the light that enters your eye and focuses a small picture onto the retina at the back of your eye. (This works in a similar way to the lens you used in the activity on page 43.) The retina sends messages about the picture to your brain. The brain sorts out the image so it looks the right way up, and you can make sense of what you see.

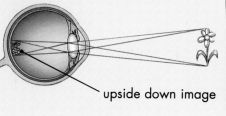

upside down image

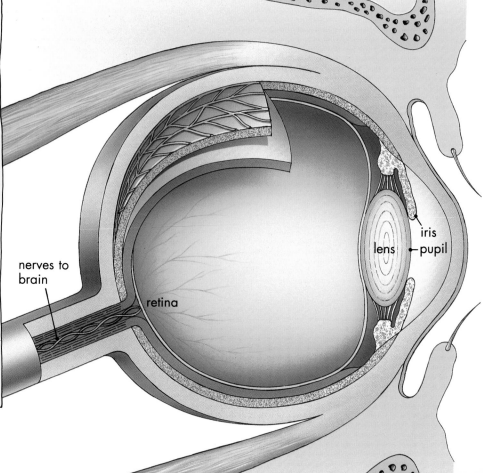

nerves to brain

retina

lens
iris
pupil

## Seeing in the Dark

Owls and cats hunt for food at night. Owls have large pupils to collect as much light as possible.

During the day, a cat's pupils are narrow slits, but at night they become wider to let in more light.

## Seeing all Around

A fly has large, dome-shaped eyes. Each eye is made up of thousands of tiny lenses and no two lenses point in the same direction. A fly can therefore see danger coming from most directions — it's almost impossible to sneak up on a fly!

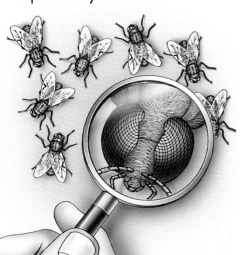

## 👁 Eye-Spy

Some people are color blind. This means that they cannot tell the difference between different colors.

For example, someone who cannot tell the difference between red and green may not be able to see the correct numbers in the circles on the right. People with normal sight read the top number as 5 and the bottom one as 8. Those with red-green color blindness may read the numbers as 2 and 3. A few people are completely color blind. They see everything in just black, white, and gray.

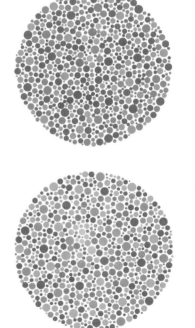

# Light of Many Colors

Although sunlight looks white, it is really made up of different colors. You can sometimes see these colors when sunlight passes through glass or water. The glass or water bends the colors by different amounts, and this makes them spread out in a rainbow pattern which we call the spectrum.

If it rains when the Sun is shining, the raindrops in the air sometimes separate the colors of sunlight and you see a rainbow in the sky.

## Rainbow Colors

A rainbow has all the colors of the spectrum — red, orange, yellow, green, blue, indigo, and violet.

## Do it yourself

**Here is an easy way to make your own rainbow.**

Lay a mirror at an angle in a dish of water. Stand the dish in front of a sunny window so that the light travels into the water and is reflected from the mirror onto some cardboard. The water covering the mirror should split the sunlight into the colors of the spectrum.

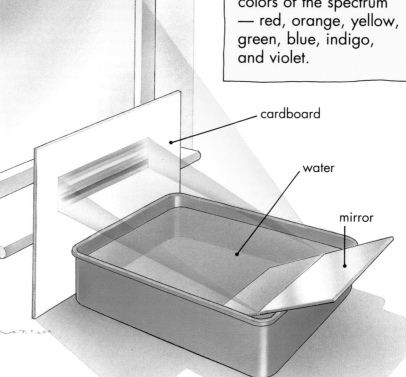

cardboard

water

mirror

## Seeing Colors

Most things do not make light of their own. They reflect light. The colors we see depend on which colors are reflected into our eyes. So a red flower looks red because it reflects more of the red part of the spectrum into our eyes than the other colors.

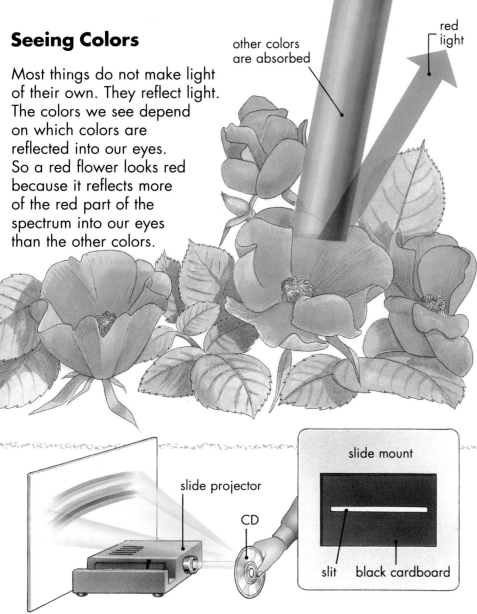

other colors are absorbed

red light

## Changing Colors

Look at the world through different colors. Shine a flashlight through colored candy wrappers, look through dyed water (food coloring works well), or buy colored light bulbs. These all filter light — a green filter only filters (lets through) green light.

slide projector

CD

slide mount

slit     black cardboard

If you hold a compact disc in front of a slide projector, you can cast lovely rainbow patterns onto white cardboard or a wall. This works best if you put a black slide with a narrow slit in it into the projector. Make one by putting two pieces of black cardboard into a slide mount. (Ask an adult to help.)

Or you could try just looking at a CD under bright light. The fine grooves in the CD reflect the light, splitting the colors into a spectrum.

47

# Bending Light

A straight straw in a glass of water looks bent. This is because light travels more slowly through water than it does through air, and when light slows down it can also change direction. This is called refraction. Glass refracts light, too. Look at some stamps through the bottom of a thick glass and see how their shape changes.

## Do it yourself

**Test refraction with this magic coin trick. You will need a glass, a coin, a marker, and some water.**

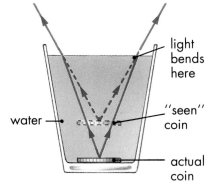

water

light bends here

"seen" coin

actual coin

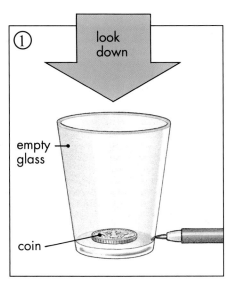

① look down

empty glass

coin

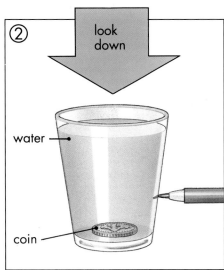

② look down

water

coin

**1.** Put a coin in the bottom of an empty glass. Look down into the glass and, at the same time, lower the marker along the side until you think it is at the same height as the coin. Were you right?

**2.** Now fill the glass with water and try the experiment again. You will probably find that you do not lower your marker far enough. This is because refraction makes the water look shallower than it really is.

# BATTERIES, BULBS, AND WIRES

# An Electric World

It's hard to imagine what life was like without electricity — no electric lights, no televisions, no computers. Yet only one hundred years ago hardly any of these things existed. Scientists could make electricity with a battery or with magnets and wires, but the first electric light bulb had only just been invented. Most people still used coal and gas to heat and light their homes.

 **Eye-Spy**

List ten things around your home that use electricity, then challenge an adult to add ten more things to your list.

In this book you'll also read about magnets. Can you think of any places where magnets are used? Perhaps you use magnets to attach messages or postcards to the door of your refrigerator.

The appliances shown below use *current* electricity. There is also a *static* electricity (see next page).

# Do it yourself

## Discover static electricity!

Rub a balloon against your sweater. This will make static electricity build up on the balloon's plastic skin. Then hold the balloon against a wall and remove your hand — the static electricity should make the balloon cling there.

**Hint:** Experiments with static electricity work best on a dry day.

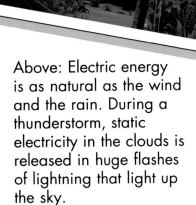

Above: Electric energy is as natural as the wind and the rain. During a thunderstorm, static electricity in the clouds is released in huge flashes of lightning that light up the sky.

rub on a sweater — wool and nylon work well

## WARNING!

The electric wires in your home are joined to the electricity supply from a power plant. They carry a huge amount of electricity and are very dangerous. So:
- **Never** use the main electricity supply for your experiments.
- **Never** go near electric pylons or cables like the ones in the photograph above.

# A First Look at Magnets

Do you have any magnets? What shape are they? Magnets come in all shapes and sizes but they all pull and push with an invisible force. And all magnets pull, or attract, some things but not others. For example, all magnets attract the metal iron. So if you use a magnet to pick up pins, it will only attract them if they contain iron.

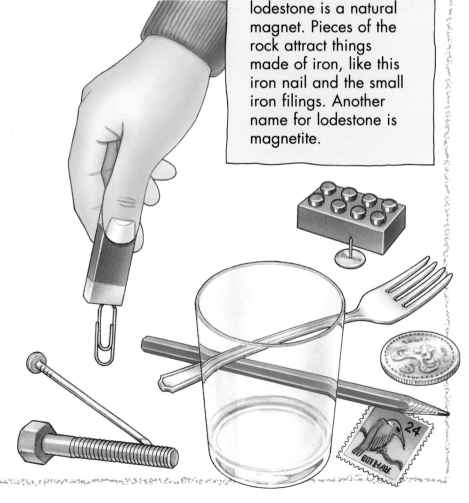

lodestone

iron filings

## Natural Magnets

The black rock called lodestone is a natural magnet. Pieces of the rock attract things made of iron, like this iron nail and the small iron filings. Another name for lodestone is magnetite.

## Do it yourself

**Test different materials, such as nails, paper clips, pins, pencils, and coins, to see whether they are magnetic. You should be able to feel the magnet's "pull" when it attracts something.**

52

# Do it yourself

## Make magnetic paper clip chains to see how strong your magnets are.

When you pick up a paper clip with a magnet, the paper clip becomes a magnet, too. You can then pick up a second paper clip on the end of the first. The stronger your magnet, the longer the chain.

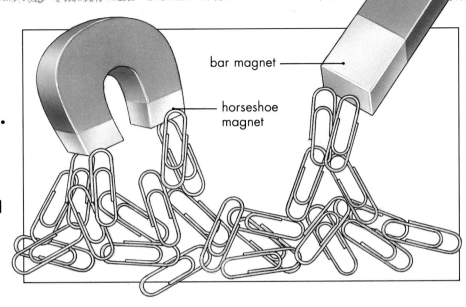

bar magnet

horseshoe magnet

## See the invisible force around your magnets.

Lay a sheet of paper over a magnet and sprinkle some iron filings on top. Gently tap the paper and see how the tiny filings are pulled into a pattern around the magnet. You could try horseshoe and circular magnets, too.

If you want to keep the patterns, ask an adult to spray the paper with glue. Shake off any loose filings when dry.

iron filings (buy from a hobby store)

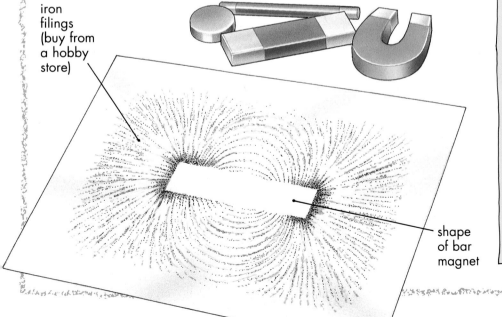

shape of bar magnet

## Magnet Poles

Every magnet has two poles. This is where the magnet's pulling force is strongest. Try pulling a nail away from different parts of a magnet to see how the force changes. If you cut a magnet in half, each piece would still have two poles — each half would be a complete magnet in itself.

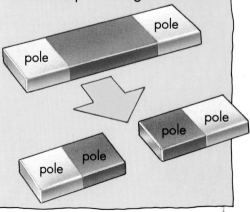

pole
pole
pole
pole
pole
pole

# Pull and Push

The two poles of a magnet are called the north pole and the south pole. This is because when a magnet swings freely it always settles with its north pole pointing toward Earth's North Pole, and its south pole pointing south. Both poles of a magnet attract iron, but the poles of different magnets do not always attract or pull toward each other. Sometimes, the poles repel each other, or push apart.

## Magnet Laws

In the experiment below, you've discovered the laws of magnets. A south pole always repels a south pole and a north pole always repels a north pole. But a north pole always attracts a south pole and a south pole always attracts a north pole.

Scientists say:
Like poles repel and unlike poles attract.

**Hint:** Some magnets have "north" and "south" labeled on them. If your magnets do not have labels, look for a tiny dent at one end. That end is the magnet's north pole.

## Do it yourself

### Test the force between the poles of two bar magnets.

Tape one of the magnets to a cork and float it on some water. Slowly bring the north pole of the second magnet toward the south pole of the floating magnet to see what happens. Make a chart like the one below and try the other combinations.

| Poles | Attract or Repel |
|-------------|------------------|
| south/north | |
| south/south | |
| north/north | |
| north/south | |

slice of cork

# Do it yourself

## Make your own magnets.

Try magnetizing an iron nail and a steel screwdriver. Make them magnetic by stroking them with a magnet at least 50 times. Always stroke the magnet across the nail or screwdriver in one direction only, and lift the magnet away after each stroke.

See how many paper clips the new magnets will pick up.

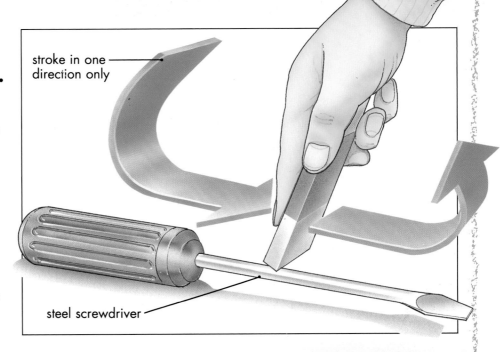

stroke in one direction only

steel screwdriver

## How It Works

Iron is made up of lots of tiny magnets that point in different directions. When the iron is magnetized, the tiny magnets all swing around to point in the same direction. This magnetism adds up, making the iron magnetic.

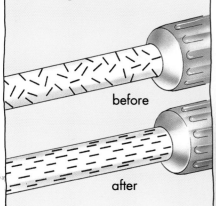

before

after

Steel is made mainly from iron and other things that harden it. The hard steel screwdriver will stay magnetic much longer than the softer iron nail. Try hitting each of them against a stone or rock to see whether they lose any of their magnetism. You will probably find that the iron nail can pick up fewer paper clips than before.

# The Pull of the Earth

Did you know that the whole Earth is magnetic? That's why a magnetic compass needle always points in the same direction — the poles of the compass needle are attracted to the Earth's North and South Poles. It's as if the Earth had a huge bar magnet inside. Scientists believe that this magnetism comes from the red-hot melted iron deep inside the Earth.

## Getting Home

Homing pigeons can sense the Earth's magnetism. They're able to find their way home after they have been released hundreds of miles away.

## Magnetic Flip

Scientists have studied the magnetism in ancient rocks. They've found that every so often the Earth's magnetic North and South Poles swap places. No one knows why this happens, or when it will happen next.

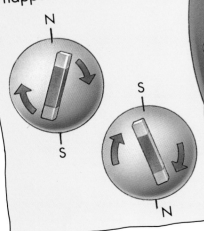

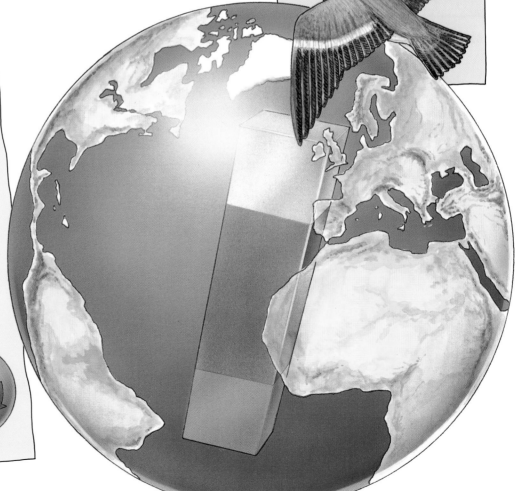

56

# Do it yourself

A compass needle swings freely and always settles down pointing north-south. To make your own compass, you'll need a magnet, a steel needle, a piece of cork, and a shallow dish.

**1.** Make the needle magnetic by stroking it with a magnet at least 50 times—in one direction only.

**2.** Place the needle on the cork and float it in a dish filled with water.

**3.** When the needle settles down, watch which direction it points in. Check the direction with a real pocket compass and label it North.

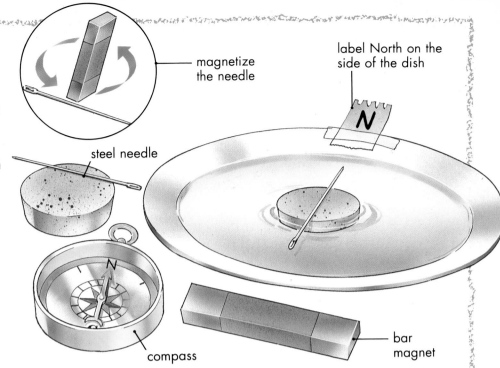

magnetize the needle

label North on the side of the dish

steel needle

N

compass

bar magnet

## Using a Compass

To use a compass, place the compass on a map and turn the map around until the North arrow points in the same direction as the compass needle.

## False Readings!

If you hold an iron nail near a compass needle, the needle will twist around as it's attracted to the iron. So don't hold a compass close to something made of iron — like a belt buckle — or you'll get a false reading!

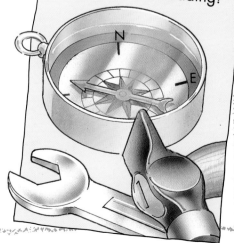

# Getting Started

The best way to learn about electricity is to experiment with it. But remember — never touch the electricity supply in your home. It can kill.

To get started, collect all the things you'll need and keep them in a box. For some activities, you'll need a buzzer and a motor. You can buy these quite cheaply from a hobby store or an electrical store.

## Basic Experiment Kit

1. Batteries (see next page)
2. Balsa wood, or cork pieces
3. Small screwdriver
4. Plastic-coated wire
5. Bulbs and bulb holders
6. Metal paper clips and thumbtacks
7. Tape

## Preparing Wire

Most wires come with a plastic coating. To join the wire to a bulb holder or to a paper clip, you must ask an adult to help you strip some of the plastic from the end so you can see the metal. Follow stages 1 to 4 which show you how to do this.

Wires can also be attached to alligator clips (right) which are then covered with plastic cases.

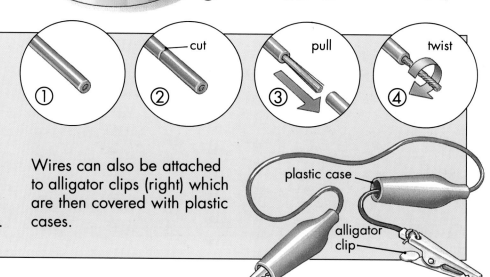

plastic case

alligator clip

## Choosing Batteries

All batteries have two terminals — a positive (+) and a negative (–). Look on the outside of your batteries to see how many volts they have.

The simplest batteries are 1.5V (one and a half volts). You can also buy 4.5V or 9V batteries. A 4.5V battery has three 1.5V cells inside it. A 9V battery has six 1.5V cells. Use 1.5V or 4.5V batteries for the experiments in this book.

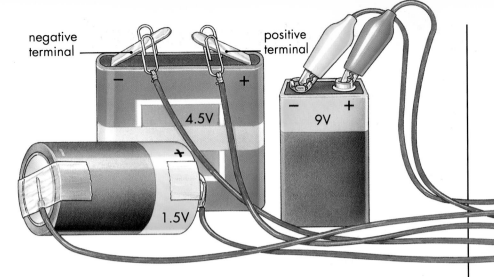

negative terminal

positive terminal

4.5V

9V

1.5V

Join the wires and batteries with tape, metal paper clips, or alligator clips. Or use a battery holder.

Whichever method you use, make sure that the metal parts touch tightly, or your experiments won't work.

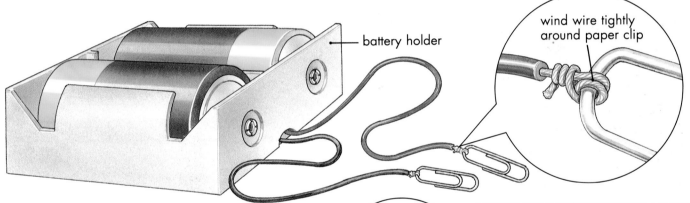

battery holder

wind wire tightly around paper clip

## Bulbs and Bulb Holders

Bulbs are made to work with a certain number of volts. This number is printed on the base of the bulb. Always use a bulb that is the same number of volts, or more volts, than your battery.

Gently screw the bulb into the holder, then screw the stripped wire under each of the holder's terminals, as shown on the right.

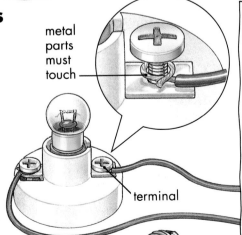

metal parts must touch

terminal

flashlight bulb

### WARNING!

- **Never** use the main electricity supply for your experiments. It can kill.
- **Never** open a battery. The chemicals inside are dangerous.
- **Always** follow the directions carefully when performing these experiments.

# Simple Circuits

To get electricity to light a bulb, it must flow around a complete path, or circuit. The battery provides the power. It pushes an electric current along the wires and through the bulb. An electric circuit works a little like the chain on your bike. When you push the pedals, your power is carried by the chain to the back wheel. If the chain breaks, the wheel won't turn. If an electric circuit is broken, the current stops flowing and the light goes out.

## Wires at Work

Connecting the tiny electric circuits in a television is very complicated. Every circuit must be complete or the TV set won't work.

## Making a Circuit

Cut two lengths of wire and strip both ends.
Connect each wire to the battery and bulb holder as shown. You can use tape, paper clips, or alligator clips, as used here.

broken circuit

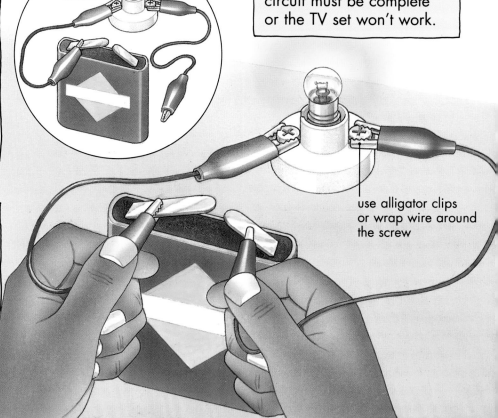

use alligator clips or wrap wire around the screw

## How It Works

The battery pushes an electric current around the circuit. The current heats the fine wire in the bulb, so it glows.

# Do it yourself

**Switches are useful because you can decide whether or not you want the electricity to flow. Make this simple switch to add to your circuit.**

**1.** Take one of the wires off the bulb holder and wrap the end tightly around a thumbtack.

**2.** Push the tack through the end of a paper clip and into a piece of balsa wood.

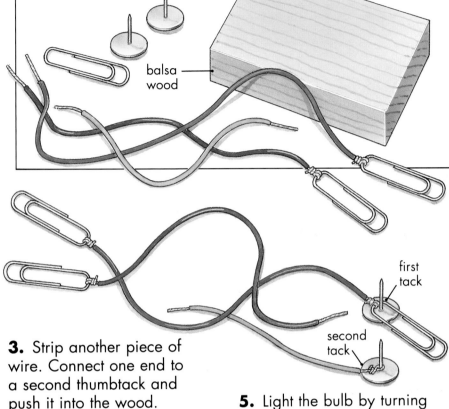

balsa wood

first tack

second tack

**3.** Strip another piece of wire. Connect one end to a second thumbtack and push it into the wood.

**4.** Connect the free end of the new wire to the free screw on the bulb holder.

**5.** Light the bulb by turning the paper clip so that it touches both tacks. Move the second thumbtack if the paper clip won't reach.

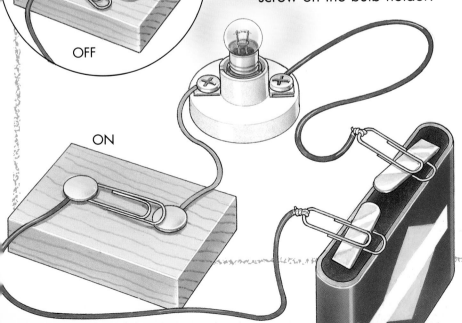

OFF

ON

## How It Works

When the switch is on, there's a complete circuit for the electricity to flow around, so the bulb lights up. When it's off, there's a break in the circuit, so the electricity can't flow and the bulb won't light.

61

# An Electric Test

Materials that carry electricity well are called conductors. Metal is a good conductor of electricity. Things that don't carry electricity are called insulators. Plastic is an insulator. Many electrical wires are covered in plastic, for safety.

## Do it yourself

**Test a collection of materials to see whether they're conductors or insulators.**

**1.** Take the switch out of your circuit so that you are left with two bare wires. If you touch the two wires together you will complete the circuit and the bulb will glow.

**2.** Touch the material to be tested with both wires. The bulb will light if the material conducts electricity. A metal nail, for example, will complete the circuit, lighting up the bulb.

**3.** Make a note of your results.

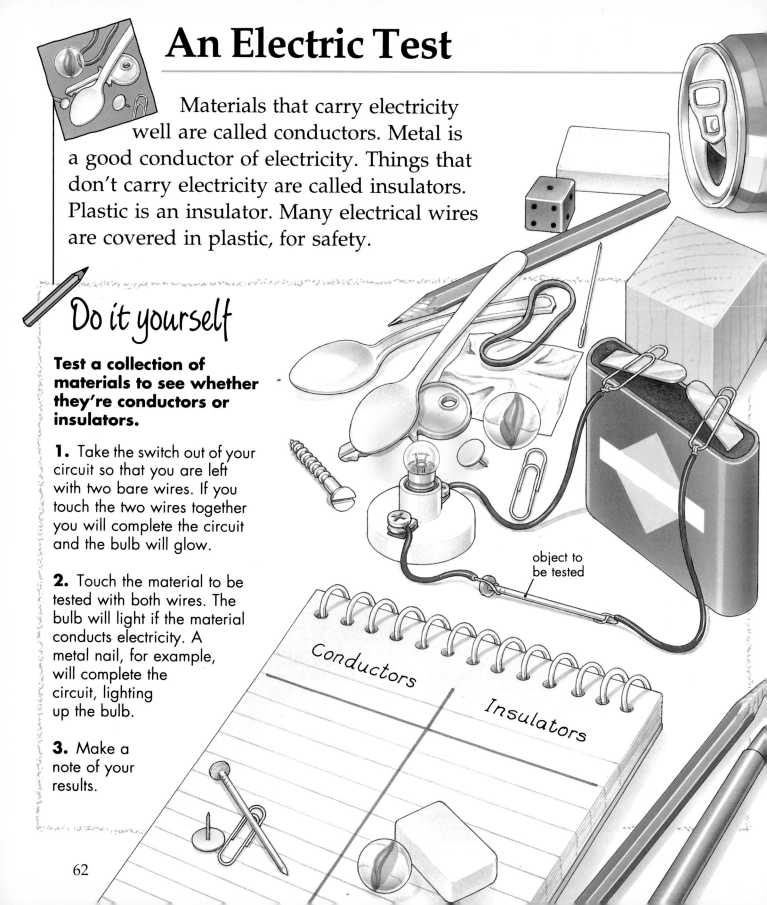

object to be tested

Conductors

Insulators

# Three Circuit Projects

Here are three circuit projects for you to try — a burglar alarm, a Morse code key, and a test of skill. For each of the projects you'll need to make a simple circuit and a special sort of switch.

## How It Works

When someone steps on them, the two pieces of cardboard touch. As they are wrapped in metal foil, they form a complete circuit, so the buzzer goes off or the bulb lights up.

## Do it yourself

**To make a burglar alarm, you will need a battery and wires, a buzzer, two plastic straws, aluminum foil, and some cardboard.**

**1.** Cut out two pieces of cardboard. Tape foil around them and make a hole in one end of each piece.

**2.** Tape the cardboard pieces together with straws in between, so that they are close but do not touch. Attach one wire to each piece of cardboard as shown.

**3.** Wire your cardboard switch in a circuit with the battery and buzzer. Use long wires so that you can hide your alarm around a corner or even in another room. Use a bulb instead of a buzzer for a silent alarm.

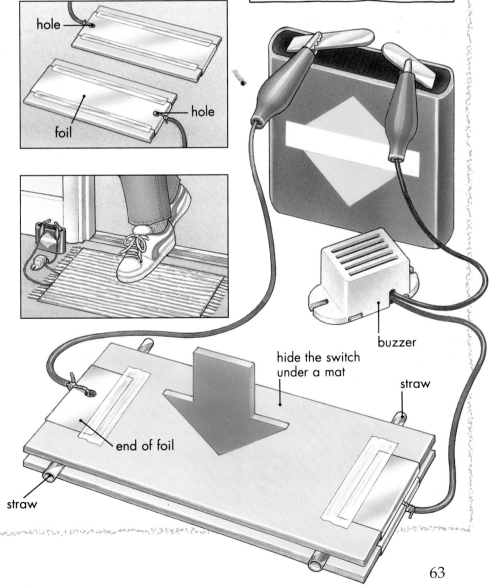

hole

hole

foil

buzzer

hide the switch under a mat

straw

end of foil

straw

# Do it yourself

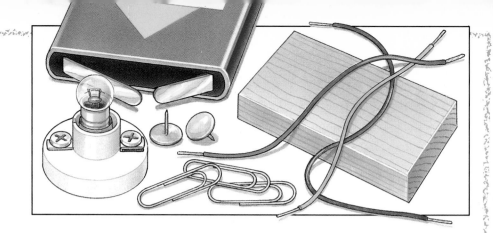

**The first messages sent by electricity were tapped out in a code of dots and dashes called Morse code. Make your own Morse code key.**

**1.** Open out a small paper clip and bend one end up. You can tape a plastic button over the raised end to make it easier to use.

**2.** Pin the paper clip to a piece of balsa wood with a thumbtack and wire the switch into a circuit. Position the second thumbtack in the balsa wood so that the raised end of the paper clip will touch it.

When you press down the paper clip it will complete the circuit, lighting up the bulb or working the buzzer.

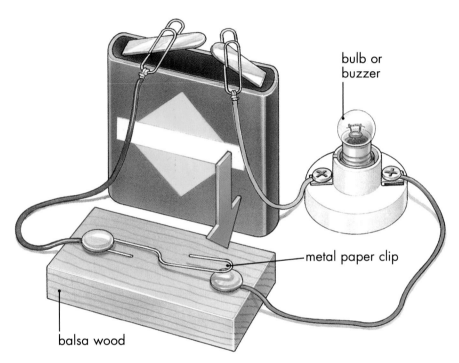

bulb or buzzer

metal paper clip

balsa wood

---

## Morse Code

The International Morse code is shown on the right. Try tapping out messages to your friends. Send a dot by tapping quickly. Send a dash by holding the paper clip down for a little longer.

| | | | | | |
|---|---|---|---|---|---|
| A | •− | B | −••• | C | −•−• |
| D | −•• | E | • | F | ••−• |
| G | −−• | H | •••• | I | •• |
| J | •−−− | K | −•− | L | •−•• |
| M | −− | N | −• | O | −−− |
| P | •−−• | Q | −−•− | R | •−• |
| S | ••• | T | − | U | ••− |
| V | •••− | W | •−− | X | −••− |
| Y | −•−− | Z | −−•• | | |

# Do it yourself

**Try this test of skill. Is your hand steady enough to take the loop from one end of the wire to the other without lighting a bulb or setting off a buzzer?**

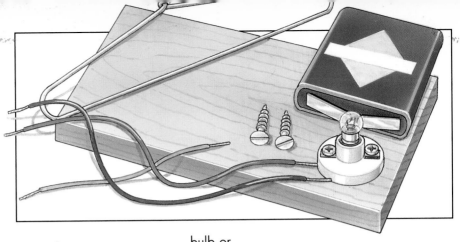

wire coathanger

bulb or buzzer

third wire

screw wire into wood

bend into loop

wooden board

first wire

second wire

## How It Works

If the looped wire touches the curved wire, the circuit will be completed so the bulb will light up or the buzzer will buzz.

**1.** Ask an adult to help you bend a wire coathanger into an interesting curved shape and screw the wire to a wooden board.

**2.** Bend the end of a shorter piece of coathanger wire into a small loop around the curvy wire on the board.

**3.** Attach one end of the first piece of stripped wire to the bottom of the short looped coathanger wire and the other end to the battery terminal.

**4.** Connect the second wire from the battery to the bulb holder and the third wire from the bulb holder to one end of the curved coathanger wire.

# Light at Night

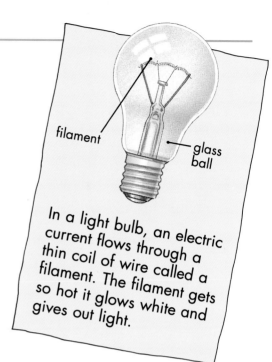

Electric lights have completely changed the way we live. We can do things at night almost as if it were still day. We can play football by floodlight and go shopping in brightly-lit shopping malls. Motorists can drive at night using car headlights, and streetlights show us the road. The centers of some big cities, like Hong Kong below, now have so many lights that astronauts can see them from space.

In a light bulb, an electric current flows through a thin coil of wire called a filament. The filament gets so hot it glows white and gives out light.

filament

glass ball

## How Light Bulbs Work

Touch the ends of two wires from a battery to a thread of fine steel wool and see how the wool glows as it is heated. When things burn, they need oxygen gas from the air. Light bulbs don't contain any oxygen, so the filament glows but does not burn away.

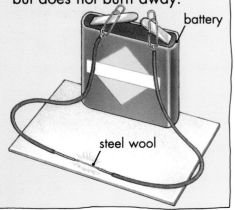

battery

steel wool

# Do it yourself

**Suppose you want to light two bulbs from just one battery. There are two ways that you can wire up the circuit — as a series circuit or as a parallel circuit.**

The two types of circuit are shown below. Wire up both kinds so that you can compare them.

The bulbs in the parallel circuit will glow more brightly than those in the series circuit.

Try taking one of the bulbs out of its holder in each circuit to see what happens to the other bulb.

series circuit — bulbs are wired as one single circuit

parallel circuit — bulbs are wired as a double circuit

## How It Works

The electricity can only flow one way in a series circuit. If you remove a bulb the circuit will be broken and the other bulb will go out.

In a parallel circuit, each bulb is wired in its own circuit. So if you remove a bulb, the electricity can still flow around the circuit and the other bulb will stay alight.

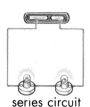

parallel circuit

series circuit

# Magnetic Links

In 1820, a scientist called Hans Oersted was experimenting with an electric circuit when he suddenly noticed that a compass needle near the wires moved when he switched the electricity on and off. He had made an important discovery — that an electric current produces magnetism.

In this MAGLEV (magnetic levitation) train, electro-magnets in the train are repelled by magnetism in the track, making the train float along.

## Do it yourself

**Try repeating Oersted's famous experiment.**

**1.** Wrap a length of wire around a cardboard tube as shown. (This makes the magnetism stronger.) Then connect the wire to a battery and a switch.

**2.** Slide a small compass into the middle of the tube.

**3.** Switch the electric circuit on and off and watch what happens to the compass needle.

## How It Works

When you switch on the circuit the electricity produces magnetism all around the wire. This attracts the compass needle and makes it swing. When the circuit is off, there is no magnetism produced so the needle goes back to its north-south position.

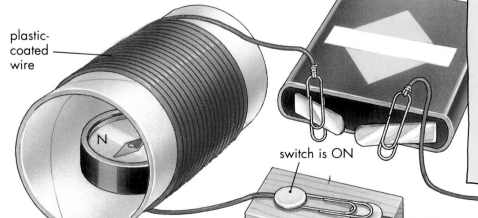

plastic-coated wire

switch is ON

# Do it yourself

**A magnet that works by electricity is called an electromagnet. Make an electromagnet with a long iron nail, wire, a battery, and a switch.**

**1.** Wind the wire around the nail, as shown. This will become your electromagnet.

**2.** Wire up the electromagnet in a circuit with the battery and the switch.

**3.** Switch on the circuit and test the magnet to see if it will pick up paper clips or pins.

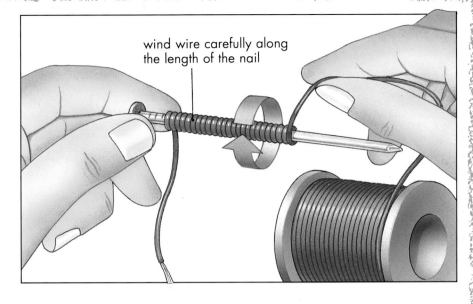

wind wire carefully along the length of the nail

The electric current in the coil of wire makes the tiny magnets inside the iron nail line up, turning the nail itself into a magnet.

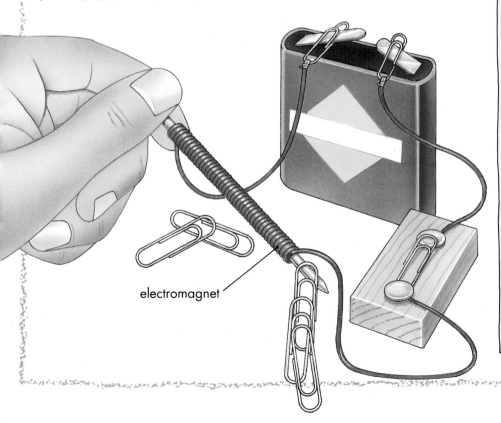

electromagnet

## More Things to Try

Try bringing one end of the electromagnet toward a compass needle to see whether the needle is attracted or repelled. Then try the same thing with the other end of the magnet.

Now change the wires around on your battery and try the same thing again. Your results should now be the other way around.

69

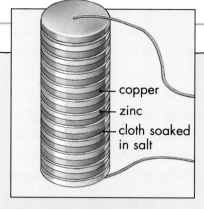

# Making Currents

Did you know that there is electricity in almost everything, but it only flows when it is given energy or power. This energy can come from the chemicals in a battery, from moving magnets, or from sunlight falling on a solar cell.

copper
zinc
cloth soaked in salt

## The First Battery

The first battery was made by Alessandro Volta in 1800. Volta discovered that when copper and zinc are stacked alternately and separated by strips of cloth soaked in salty water or an acid, an electric current flows between them.

## Do it yourself

### Try making a simple battery with vinegar.

**1.** Fill three small glass jars with vinegar (an acid).

**2.** Wrap bare copper wire around two galvanized (zinc-coated) nails, and link jars 1 and 2, and 2 and 3 as shown.

**3.** Put a third nail in jar 3 and a third piece of wire in jar 1. These are your battery's terminals.

**4.** Connect the terminals to an LED and you should see it light up.

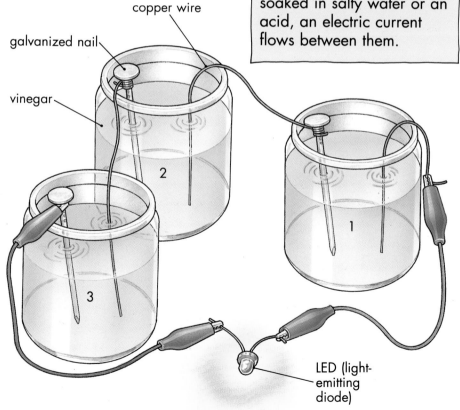

copper wire
galvanized nail
vinegar

LED (light-emitting diode)

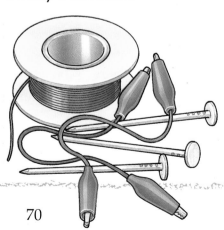

# SOLIDS AND LIQUIDS

# What's It Made Of?

Have you ever wondered what makes one thing different from another? A ball, a drop of water, the wind, are all very different because they are made from different materials.

Most materials are solid, such as metal and wood. Solids don't change shape unless you cut, bend, or break them. Some solids, like glass, break easily. Some, like stone and many plastics, are very strong.

Other materials are liquid. Water is a liquid. It flows and doesn't have a shape of its own.

Solids don't last forever. Glass breaks easily. Cloth and paper rot. Stone wears away, and some metals rust.

### 👁 Eye-Spy

Make a collection of different solids and decide whether they are made of wood, metal, plastic, stone, rubber, glass, or something else.

Here are five solid materials that look and feel different.
**1.** Metals are strong. They can be sharpened into blades for cutting.

A third kind of material is gas. Air is a gas. You can't see it and it is so thin you can pass your hand through it. Yet you can feel air when it blows over your face and hands.

**2.** Rubber is light and grips well. It is also springy and returns to its original shape when it is stretched.

**3.** Glass is transparent (you can see through it), but it breaks if you drop it.

**4.** Most clothes are woven from fibers (fine threads). Woven fibers are strong and flexible — they bend easily.

**5.** Plastic is strong, light, and waterproof. It doesn't rot or rust and it can be made into any shape.

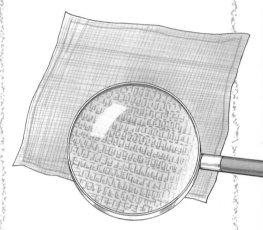
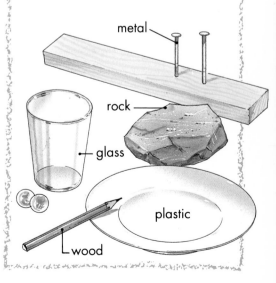

# Materials All Around

Everything we use is made from materials. Some, like cotton, come from plants. Others, like wool, come from animals. Many buildings are made from stone which is cut or dug from the ground. Cotton, wool, and stone are all natural materials.

Some natural materials can be made into other things. Oil can be made into plastics. Coal can be made into paint or soap. Coal and oil are called raw materials. Plastic is a manufactured, or artificial, material.

All plants and animals are made from many different materials. Two of the main ones are water and carbon. (Carbon is the black stuff in the middle of pencils.) In every human body there is enough water to fill 4 buckets and enough carbon to make over 1,000 pencils.

## Wood into Coal

**1.** Millions of years ago the Earth was covered by thick forests and swamps.
**2.** Fallen trees were gradually buried by thick layers of mud and sand.
**3.** The squashed wood slowly turned into coal.

Oil is formed from the remains of ancient plants and animals. We drill for oil and dig for coal under the Earth's surface, through layers of rock.

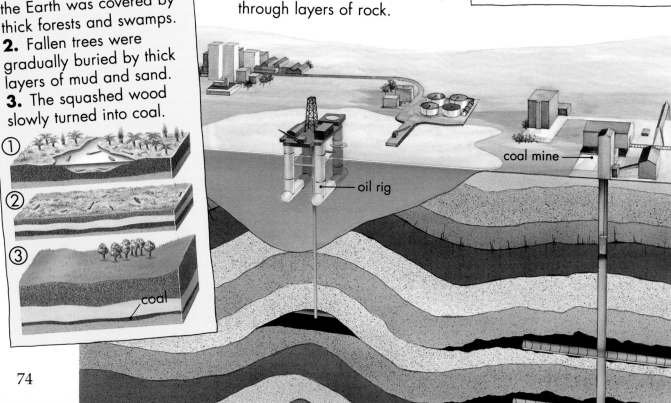

coal mine

oil rig

coal

One of the main gases that makes up air is oxygen. All living things need oxygen. We must breathe oxygen gas to stay alive. Plants "breathe out" lifegiving oxygen.

When materials like coal and oil burn they use oxygen from the air and give out heat (see next page).

nitrogen (78%)
oxygen (21%)
carbon dioxide (0.03%)
argon and other gases (0.97%)

## What's in Air?

Air is mostly made up of the two gases nitrogen and oxygen. It also contains water in the form of a gas (water vapor) and tiny bits of salt, dust, and dirt.

# Do it yourself

**See how materials use oxygen when they burn. You'll need a small candle, a saucer, some water, and a glass jar.**

**1.** Ask an adult to stick the candle to the bottom of the saucer with some melted candle wax, and then light the candle for you.

**2.** Pour about half an inch (1 cm) of water into the bottom of the saucer. Turn a glass jar upside down and carefully lower it over the candle. The glass should just sit in the water. Watch what happens to the candle flame.

watch the candle flame

saucer or jar lid
glass
water level

## How It Works

The candle needs oxygen gas to burn. It therefore goes out when it has used up most of the oxygen in the glass. The water rises in the glass to take the space of the used oxygen.

# Melting and Mixing

Have you ever sat in front of a roaring log fire? The wood on the fire uses oxygen as it burns. The burning wood gives off heat and turns into ash.

Heat changes materials. It can change solids into liquids and liquids into gases. Heat can make things melt, make them cook, and set them on fire.

### 👁 Eye-Spy

See how chocolate melts and goes runny on a hot day — it changes from a solid to a liquid.

## Do it yourself

**Find out how heat affects different materials. You will need three saucers, some ice, a chocolate bar, some butter, and a wax candle.**

Arrange a piece of each material around the edges of the saucers (You'll need three pieces of each material.) Put one saucer in the refrigerator, one in a cool room, and one in sunlight or next to a hot fire.

- Which materials melt?

- Which go soft?

- Which stay solid?

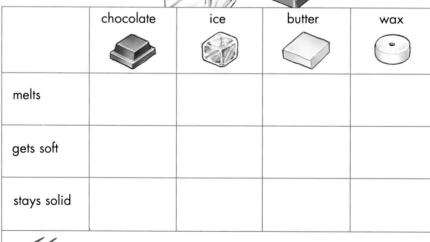

|  | chocolate | ice | butter | wax |
|---|---|---|---|---|
| melts |  |  |  |  |
| gets soft |  |  |  |  |
| stays solid |  |  |  |  |

✔✔ hot spot
✔ cool room
● refrigerator

You could use a chart like this to record your results. Try testing some other materials in the same way.

# Do it yourself

**See how some liquids will mix together while others don't mix at all, and how some solids dissolve (mix into a liquid).**

## Mixing

Stir some milk into hot coffee to see how the milk and coffee mix to a brown color. Now try dropping a blob of ink or food coloring into some water to see how they mix together.

## Unmixing

Pour equal amounts of cooking oil and water into a clear plastic jar with a screw-on top. Screw on the top and shake the jar hard to try and mix the contents together. Leave the bottle to stand and watch how the oil floats on top of the water in a layer.

## Dissolving

When you stir sugar into a hot drink it dissolves. Most things dissolve more easily in warm water than in cold. Try stirring the things on the right into hot and then cold water and see what happens.

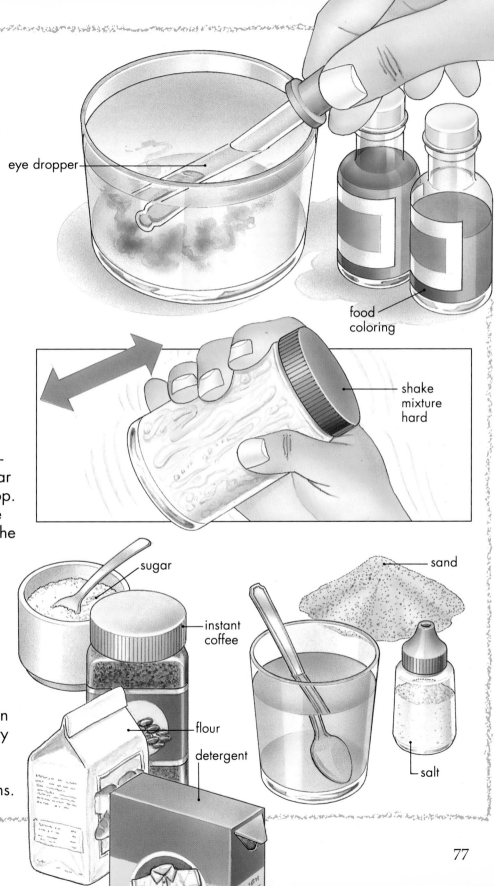

eye dropper

food coloring

shake mixture hard

sugar

instant coffee

sand

flour

detergent

salt

77

# Mixing Things Together

All solids, liquids, and gases are made up of chemicals. When some chemicals are mixed together they react, or change, and new chemicals are made.

Did you know that cooking is a kind of chemical reaction? When you bake a cake in the oven all the things you put into the mixture react together to make a solid. Beating the cake mixture is important because it mixes in air — it's the air bubbles that make the cake light and fluffy.

## Chemistry

Chemistry is the name for the part of science that is all about what things are made of and how they can be changed.

### 👁 Eye-Spy

Ask an adult to boil some red cabbage and then help you to pour off some of the cabbage water into two dishes. Add lemon juice to one dish and baking powder to the second. See how the chemical reactions make the water change color.

red cabbage water on its own

with baking powder

with lemon juice

# Do it yourself

**Warning! You must do this experiment outside. It can be very messy!**

**Make a chemical reaction that will power a rocket. You'll need a small plastic bottle with a screw-on top, a long piece of smooth string, a plastic straw, tape, tissue paper, vinegar, and baking powder.**

**1.** Thread the string through the straw and stretch it out as shown. Pour an inch of vinegar into the bottle and tape the bottle to the straw.

**2.** Put a few teaspoonfuls of baking powder into some tissue paper and wrap it into a parcel.

**3.** Gently slide the parcel into the bottle, trying to keep it out of the vinegar until you have screwed on the top of the bottle.

**4.** Give the bottle a shake and wait for takeoff!

thin string

small plastic bottle

make a small hole in bottle top (ask an adult to help)

vinegar

tissue paper

baking powder

straw

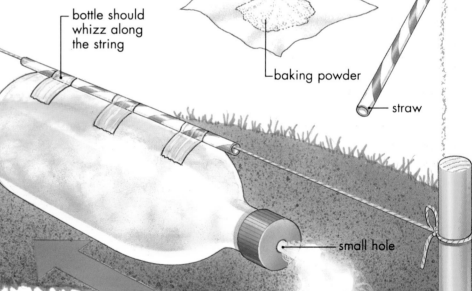

string stretched tightly between two posts

bottle should whizz along the string

small hole

## How It Works

When baking powder and vinegar mix together there is a chemical reaction and carbon dioxide gas is made. As more and more gas is made, the pressure builds up inside the bottle, shooting the gas out of the hole and pushing the bottle along the string.

79

# Making Tools

Long ago, people chipped flints from huge stones and used them to make arrows, spearheads, and sharp blades for knives and axes. Their tools did similar jobs to tools we use today, but they were more clumsy and harder to handle.

## Do it yourself

**Try making your own tools with sticks, stones, and strong string.**

You could use pebbles to make hammerheads. Sticks can be cut into tool handles or digging sticks. But be careful — ask an adult to help you cut them.

If you live in a chalky area, you may be able to find pieces of flint. Flint is a glassy, hard stone found in some rocks. You could then try making a flint ax or scraper like the ones shown here.

Try doing different jobs with your tools. Are they easy to use?

## Metal Tools

Most modern tools have sharp, light metal blades. Some have motors to make them work faster.

scraper

flint ax

put stone in fork of a branch and bind the wood around it with string

hammer

digging stick

stick

stones

strong string

Later, people began to make better tools from metals. They discovered a way of heating certain types of rocks so they could get copper out of them. Then they found that when they mixed tin with the hot copper it made a new material — bronze.

Copper and tin are quite soft and flexible on their own, but bronze is hard enough to be used for sharp knife blades and ax heads.

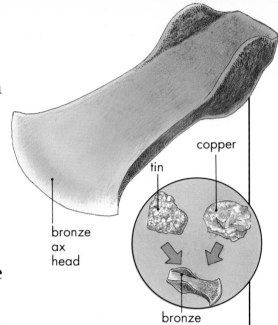

copper

tin

bronze
ax
head

bronze

## The Bronze Age

The Bronze Age started about 5,000 years ago. Bronze tools and ornaments have been found in the Middle East, China, and Europe.

## The Iron Age

About 3,000 years ago people found a way of separating iron from rocks. Iron is stronger than bronze. Iron tools last longer and can be sharpened more easily.

### 👁 Eye-Spy

Visit a museum and look out for stone, bronze, and iron tools and weapons. You'll find that the wooden handles have rotted away.

# Metal Magic

We now use more than fifty kinds of metal and most of them are found in rocks. Some of the more common ones are iron, copper, tin, aluminum, silver, gold, and chromium. As each type of metal has different properties it can be used in different ways. Some metals are better for making cars and others for making coins.

### Strong Metal

Steel is very strong. Steel wires and girders are often used to make bridges. Steel is mainly iron with a small amount of carbon mixed in it to make the iron stronger and harder.

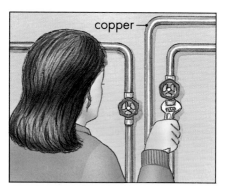

### Flexible Metal

Pure metals (metals that have not been mixed with anything else) are quite soft and bendy. They are used for wires or pipes.

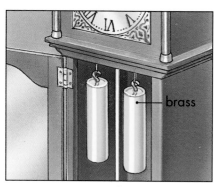

### Heavy Metal

Nearly all metals are heavier than water, so they sink. Lead and brass are two of the heaviest metals. They are often used to make weights.

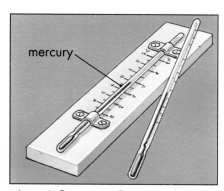

### Liquid Metal

All metals melt into thick liquids when they get very hot. Mercury is special. It is the only metal that stays liquid when it is cool.

# Do it yourself

**Use these four tests to help you decide whether something is made from metal.**

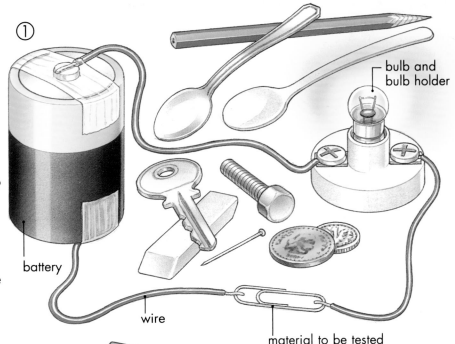

bulb and bulb holder

battery

wire

material to be tested

## 1. Does it carry electricity?
Test your material with a battery, a bulb, and two wires. All metal conducts, or carries, electricity. For the test to work, the wires must touch bare metal, not paint.

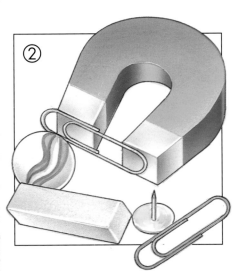

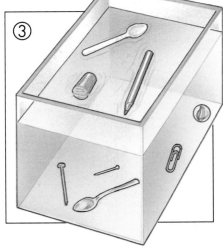

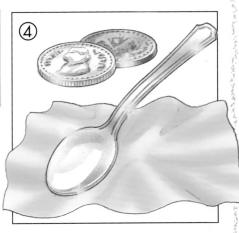

## 2. Is it magnetic?
If your material is attracted or "pulled" by a magnet, then it contains the metal iron. If not, then it may still be a metal like copper or aluminum (which aren't magnetic).

## 3. Does it float or sink?
All common metals are heavier than water, so they will sink. Therefore, if your material floats on water it is not a metal and must be made from something else.

## 4. Can it be polished?
Most metals can be polished to a bright shine. Metals shine in light so they can be used as mirrors. If you can see through your material, then it isn't a metal.

# Useful Plastics

Plastics are not natural materials. They're made in factories from the chemicals found in oil. The chemicals are heated in steel tanks which are rather like huge pressure cookers. When the chemicals stick together, new plastic materials are made.

Plastics are lighter and more flexible than metals, but they aren't as strong. Plastics can melt or burn when they are heated. An important property of plastic is that it doesn't conduct electricity, so plastic is wrapped around electric wire to make the wire safer.

Plastic gets soft when it's heated, so it can be made into all sorts of shapes, like these toys.

## Eye-Spy

Put a yogurt container in a bowl. Then ask an adult to pour some very hot water over it. Watch how the plastic container softens and changes shape.

boiling water

yogurt container

Plastic canoes and safety helmets don't crack or shatter when they get knocked.

# Do it yourself

## Make some rubbery plastic at home from milk and vinegar.

**1.** Ask an adult to warm some creamy milk in a pan. When the milk is simmering, slowly stir in a few teaspoonfuls of vinegar.

creamy milk

vinegar

wash in cold water

**2.** Keep stirring, but just before the mixture becomes rubbery add some food coloring.

**3.** Let the plastic cool and wash it under cold running water.

## Stretchy, Strong, or Brittle?

Find some different kinds of plastic and try bending and stretching them. Are they stretchy and weak or stretchy and strong? Or are they brittle (do they snap easily)?

plastic spoon

homemade plastic

plastic can holders

plastic wrap

# Flexible Fibers

Fibers are simply long, thin, flexible strands or threads. We use both natural fibers, from plants and animals, and artificial fibers, from oil and coal. Cotton comes from the seed pods of the cotton plant and wool comes from sheep. String can be made from plant fibers, and nylon is made from the chemicals in oil.

Plant, animal, and artificial fibers can all be woven to make different kinds of cloth. Look at the labels in your clothes. Some will be made from mixtures of fibers, like cotton and nylon, or cotton and polyester.

A hair is a fiber. Animal fur is just a thick coat of hair. It traps tiny pockets of air between the fibers, keeping in the warmth.

### 👁 Eye-Spy

Collect some different fibers and look at them through a magnifying glass. Are they smooth or rough, thick or thin? Wool and string are much rougher than nylon.

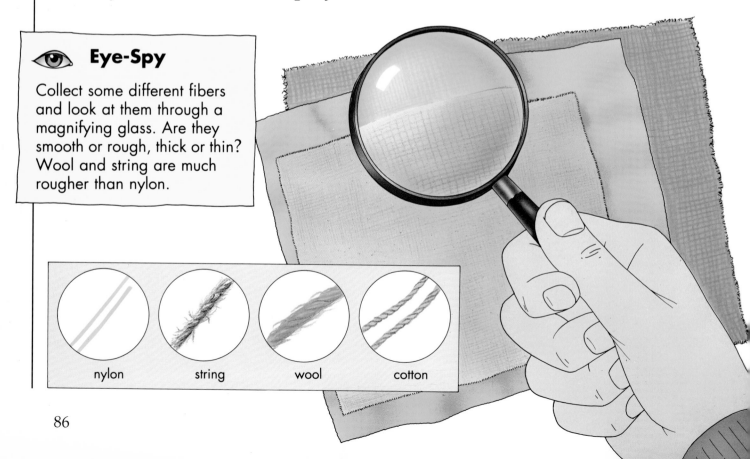

nylon    string    wool    cotton

Paper is made from fibers, too. Usually it's made from wood fibers. The wood is separated into fibers by crushing it to a pulp in water. The pulp is then squeezed into thin sheets and dried.

If you look at a piece of cloth and a piece of tissue paper under a magnifying glass you can see the fibers clearly. The fibers in cloth are woven together evenly. But the fibers in paper are just squashed together in a jumble.

secure with rubber band

yogurt container

## Making It Waterproof

Cloth is not usually waterproof because of all the tiny holes between the fibers. Try making a piece of cloth waterproof by rubbing it with candle wax to block the holes. See if it has worked by wrapping the cloth around the top of a container filled with water then tipping the container upside down.

# Do it yourself

**Try weaving a piece of cloth with some yarn.**

**1.** Cut a row of triangular grooves in opposite sides of a piece of thick cardboard.

**2.** Wind the yarn around the cardboard as shown. This is called the warp.

**3.** Thread the needle with another strand of wool and weave it in and out of the warp thread. This is the weft.

**4.** When you've finished, knot the end and cut the threads so that you can remove the cardboard.

stiff cardboard

warp

weft

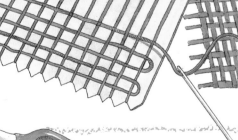

# Strong But Brittle

Glass is made from sand — just like the sand on a beach. The sand is heated with limestone and other materials until they melt and mix together. The red-hot mixture is poured into different shapes. It then cools and sets to solid glass.

Glass is a very useful material. As it's transparent, we use it for windows and glasses. It's also waterproof and easy to clean, so it is used to make bottles and jars.

**Breaking Glass**

Although glass is strong and hard, it is also brittle. This means that it can shatter easily. A glass bottle can carry a heavy weight without breaking, but a sudden knock can make it shatter. Have you ever dropped a glass and seen it break into sharp pieces? (Don't test this out though, you could hurt yourself!)

When broken glass is especially dangerous, a special safety glass is used.

Left: Some glass bowls or ornaments are made by glass blowers. They pick up a blob of soft glass on the end of a hollow tube. Then they blow into the tube and the glass blows up like a balloon.

# Making It Strong

A tennis racket must be strong enough to hit a ball without breaking. A bridge needs be able to take the weight of all the traffic that uses it. Things must be made so that they are safe and strong enough to last. To make something strong, you must use a strong material and you must make it into a strong shape.

### Wonderful Webs

The silken strands in a spider's web are just 0.0001 inch thick but they are stronger than steel of the same thickness!

## Concrete Strength

Many buildings are made out of concrete, which is a mixture of cement, water, and gravel or sand. As concrete can crack if it is stretched, it is often reinforced (made stronger) by thin steel rods that are set into the mixture.

## Safety Glass

Car windshields are usually made of safety glass. The glass may still shatter but the pieces won't fly into the driver's face because they're held in place by a sheet of clear plastic sandwiched between two glass sheets.

## Carbon Fibers

Fibers made from carbon are flexible, light, and strong. They are used to make parts of bikes, tennis rackets, and aircraft bodies. Carbon fibers weigh about a quarter as much as steel, but they are twice as strong.

# Do it yourself

## See if you can design a strong bridge shape.

**1.** First try experimenting with paper bridge shapes. Paper is much too flexible to make a flat bridge, but if you fold the paper the bridge can be made much stiffer and stronger. Three strong bridge shapes are shown below.

Above: Sydney Harbour Bridge in Australia is made from steel. It carries eight lanes of traffic and two railroad tracks.

**2.** Try making a bridge frame out of plastic straws. Join the straws by pushing the end of one into the end of another, then taping them together. You can test your bridge's strength by seeing whether it can take the weight of a yogurt container filled with sand.

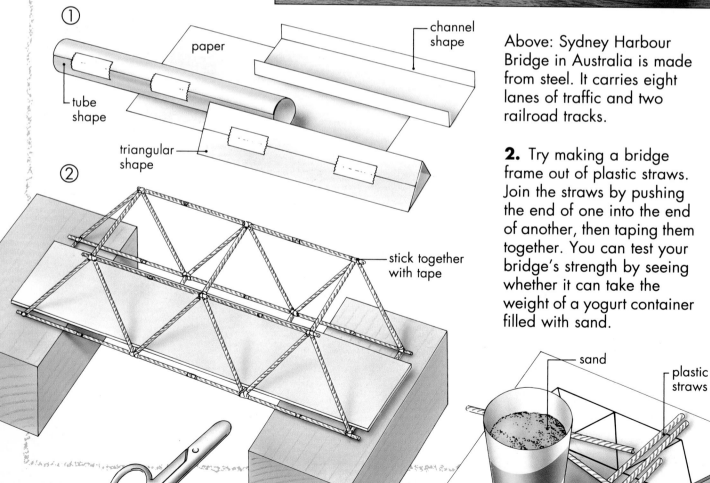

① paper

channel shape

tube shape

triangular shape

② stick together with tape

sand

plastic straws

# Using It Again

Have you ever counted how many glass bottles, metal cans, or plastic containers are thrown away in your house in a week, or a month? It all adds up to a lot of garbage.

Instead of throwing away glass, metal, and plastic, you can help the environment by using them again. Recyling reduces the amount of garbage we make and saves energy and money.

## New From Old

This recycling plant in Germany sorts out different metals. The steel will be reused to make new containers.

## Do it yourself

### See which things rot away.

Dig a hole and bury a soda can, a glass jar, a plastic container, paper, and some apple slices. Mark the place with a stick. Dig it up after two weeks.

Don't forget to take your garbage away after two weeks is up!

### How It Works

Worms and other tiny creatures will have begun to eat the food and paper. These things are biodegradable. The glass, plastic, and metal would just lie in the soil for years.

# Do it yourself

**Recycle the things you use. Every little bit helps so if you don't already recycle your garbage — start now!**

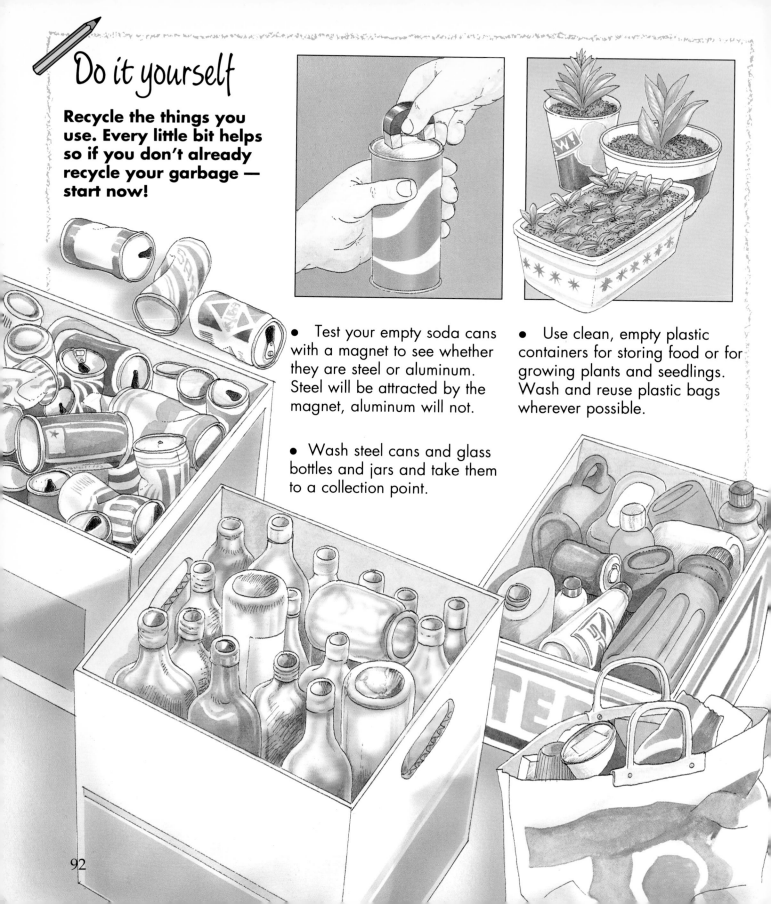

● Test your empty soda cans with a magnet to see whether they are steel or aluminum. Steel will be attracted by the magnet, aluminum will not.

● Wash steel cans and glass bottles and jars and take them to a collection point.

● Use clean, empty plastic containers for storing food or for growing plants and seedlings. Wash and reuse plastic bags wherever possible.

# Index

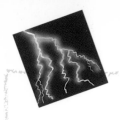

**Photographs:**
Heather Angel; Christine Osborne Pictures; David Glover; Hutchison Library (Andrew Hill); J. Allan Cash Ltd; Kanehara Shipping Co. Ltd; Life File Photo Library; NHPA; Robert Harding Picture Library; Science Photo Library (Taheshi Tokahora); ZEFA

Every effort has been made to trace the copyright holders of the photographs. The publishers apologize for any inconvenience caused.